Praise for ***The Green Edge***

"Tom Bowman has cemented his position as the premier expert on sustainability for the event industry with *The Green Edge*. This book provides event managers and planners with a practical guide to sustainability practices that result in real gains while adhering to good sound business practices. A must read for event marketing professionals who are serious about defining or refining their sustainability strategy."

—Skip Cox, President and CEO
Exhibit Surveys, Inc.

"Tom Bowman's book is important for the meeting and event business. Tom offers practical advice on how to use green thinking to save money and produce better events. We need more books like this."

—Andrew Winston, Bestselling Author
Green to Gold* and *The Big Pivot

"Events are such a big part of what every business does, but finding greener ways to create them is so challenging. This book makes it easy. Even better, it helps companies live their brand values."

—Elysa Hammond, Director of Environmental Stewardship
Clif Bar & Company

"*The Green Edge* is as useful as a Swiss Army Knife, packed with case studies, resources, metrics and much more. It has 1,001 uses, but above all, by the time you finish you'll know how to add green to your bottom line by going green."

—Charles Pappas, Senior Writer
***EXHIBITOR* Magazine**

"Our sector of the industry was just handed our roadmap or, better yet, our owner's manual. At the same time, *The Green Edge* is also a terrific read, not pedantic and academic, but rather conversational and easy to follow."

—Jeff Provost, Executive Director
Exhibit Designers and Producers Association

"Tom Bowman has demonstrated that green business is good business. Now he has written a guidebook to lead the very large meetings and events industry to a more successful future. *The Green Edge* outlines business strategies that save money and build stronger companies, and that's a winning combination."

—Susan Frank, President and COO
Better World Group

"Bowman's new book *The Green Edge* is an important contribution to the growing literature on sustainability. The book's value extends far beyond the domain of exhibit designers and meeting planners. I recommend it highly."

—Jerry Schubel, President and CEO
Aquarium of the Pacific

"The Exhibit and Event Marketers Association applauds the fine job Tom Bowman has done to raise awareness of green exhibiting."

—Jim Wurm, Executive Director
Exhibit and Event Marketers Association

The Green Edge

The Green Edge

HOW SUSTAINABILITY CAN HELP EXHIBIT AND MEETING PLANNERS SAVE MONEY AND BUILD STRONGER BRANDS

Tom Bowman

BGC
Signal Hill, CA

The Green Edge

How Sustainability Can Help Exhibit and Meeting Planners
Save Money and Build Stronger Brands

By Tom Bowman

©2014 Thomas E. Bowman
BGC, 1870 Obispo Ave, Signal Hill, CA 90755

All rights reserved. No part of this publication may be reproduced or transmitted in any form or by any means, electronic or mechanicaly, including photocopy, or any information storage and retrieval system, without permission from the publisher.

Cover design by Ed Hackley

First edition softcover

ISBN 978-0-9915703-0-0

Printed in the United States

My father taught me not to think of obstacles as barriers.
Tina taught me that time flies when you're having fun.

Contents

Preface

Nobody writes business books addressed to you. You work in an industry that is populated by middle managers on the client side and small businesses on the supplier side. When was the last time you saw a bestselling title written for people in your position? It's a shame not to acknowledge what a difference you can make, and help you overcome the barriers that are holding you back. We both know what they are. I also know that you are coming to this issue with interest, and with a few myths that deserve to get busted. It just makes sense to address a book to us.

I once read a surprising estimate that there are 500,000 to 1 million meeting and event managers in North America alone, so you can imagine what the global tally must be. I can't begin to estimate how many industry suppliers, event organizers and others support the work you do on the client side, but the numbers must be huge. And here's the thing: Meetings and event managers work in every conceivable industry, market and type of organization. Businesses have them, cultural institutions have them, government agencies and non-governmental organizations have them, as do the professions. It would be hard to imagine a more crosscutting middle management activity in society than this one.

I've been in this business for a long time, some 30 years, most of it as the owner of a small company on the supplier side. I've been an exhibitor as well, which opened my eyes to a whole new perspective on the choices you make. I also attend a great many professional and industry conferences that have very little to do with trade shows. I've seen the professional pride and jealousies that make people think trade shows, museums and professional conferences are different worlds, but they truly are not. All three segments share the same challenges, management practices and even the same suppliers. We think of trade shows as flashy, loud and highly commercial, and they certainly are. In contrast, we think of professional conferences as quiet and somewhat more dignified, and this also is true. But if you step back a bit, you realize that trade shows often have conferences attached to them, and that professional conferences often have exhibits somewhere on a show floor. You and I work at the epicenter of these activities. We are all in this soup together.

Yet nobody writes books that address the world we work in. A lot of business titles read like self-help books with practical dos and don'ts cherry-picked from a few case studies. Best practices catch on this way: One group does something unexpected and it works, everyone jumps on the bandwagon and it becomes the latest trend. I'm not just talking about the business community here because the same thing happens in the museum world and elsewhere. Let's face it: Professionals like you are always looking for ways to do better.

A journal editor once asked how to engage the public in sustainability. The answer seems obvious: Look at the places where people work on changing things. If you want to engage people in sustainability, go see the people who want to do it.

Businesses are competitive problem-solving enterprises that move like lightning when they see opportunities. When that happens, the people in your position do most of the heavy lifting. Why not start with you? On the question of sustainability, a lack of useful, practical information seemed to be holding all of us back. So I set out to address the glaring need to give industry professionals the practical information and tools to solve our eco-challenges: carbon, pollution, conservation, waste and more.

Some of us go looking for answers in the nonfiction business classics—such as *Good to Great*, *Green to Gold* and *The Triple Bottom Line*—hoping to glean insights, but it takes some doing and some authority to apply those insights to your job. It helps to be an executive, of course, because people write books for them. But nobody writes for us: the 500,000 to 1-million middle managers, small business suppliers and our enormous global cohort. Nobody writes to us. Nobody writes about us. Nobody points out how to achieve winning breakthroughs in the work we actually do.

When you see a gap in a market and an unfulfilled need, what do you do? If you're interested in marketing or education or business, you look for ways to fill it. I hope this book helps you get off the sidelines. Achieving genuine sustainability is an exciting challenge, and I wish you the best of luck in the game.

Tom Bowman
Signal Hill, California
February 2014

Introduction

Are you confused about "going green"? Have you been directed to make your events program more sustainable? Are you just getting your feet wet, and wonder whether it's right for you? Perhaps you have taken some initial steps but have gotten frustrated. Do you want to go green because it matters to you personally? Is sustainability part of your brand's lifeblood? Is your company feeling pressured by competitors or outside groups? There are many reasons to take the sustainability plunge. In its 2013 survey of 1600 global companies, GreenBiz.com summarized, "We do these things not because they are required by law, but because they make us a better company. They reduce costs, improve quality, meet customers' expectations, engage employees, and foster innovative new products and services. They help improve the bottom line and, in some cases, grow the top line."[1]

But there are risks, too, that keep many meeting organizers and exhibitors from diving in. Perhaps you've seen enough "greenwashing" to be wary. Greenwashing is the practice of slapping a sustainability label on a product or service that offers little or no environmental benefit. We've all seen it; that's how Chevrolet's heavy SUV, the Tahoe Hybrid, became the Los Angeles Auto Show's Green Car of the Year in 2007.[2] Sure, the hybrid version of the Tahoe got 25 percent better gas mileage than its gasoline-powered cousins, but at 20 miles per gallon[3] it was hardly blazing a trail compared to the national average for new cars that year. These rather obvious facts led many people to conclude that the Green Car of the Year award was less of a nod to environmental leadership than a splash of greenwash.

Perhaps you are concerned that you'll just end up chasing green myths. Given how quickly popular ideas can spread and become accepted wisdom, you are wise to be wary. One often repeated story says the U.S. Environmental Protection Agency determined that "trade shows are the second biggest source of commercial waste in the United States."[4] But no such federal report has ever been written.

Yet green myths persist. For example, contrary to often-published, green business advice, lightweight exhibits do almost nothing to improve a heavy-duty truck's fuel economy and reduce air pollution. Slashing weight will save dollars on your drayage bills, of course, but that is a separate issue. If "lightweight" happens also to mean, "fits into a smaller package so that more exhibits can be loaded onto the truck," then the purported environmental benefits are real. It's volume, not weight, that matters if you want to reduce air pollution from shipping your exhibits to trade shows.[5]

And green myths are plentiful. One says that banning plastic shopping bags is a great way to fight climate change. Sadly, the amount of carbon pollution that can be eliminated this way is almost too small to measure.[6] Another says eating locally sourced foods is the best way to cut those same emissions. But the truth is quite different: Running yourself ragged trying to find locally produced foods for your next catered event will barely make a dent in your carbon budget. Local sourcing is a good way to support the community's economy, of course, but you can slice and dice greenhouse gas emissions more effectively by making much easier food choices.[7]

That's not to suggest that these actions are meaningless. In fact, there are good reasons to do many of the things that green myths advise. Banning plastic bags, for example, reduces roadside litter, and shopping locally is great for the farmers and their neighbors. But when actions such as these are pitched as important, climate-friendly choices, as they so often are, they become little more than distracting and easily debunked myths. And it's that fear of being duped by these misrepresentations that makes so many cautious managers reluctant to dive in.

Perhaps the biggest myth of all says that going green costs more money. One exhibit house owner I know tells his clients that if a new exhibit will cost $100,000, then a new green exhibit will cost $150,000. That would turn any reasonable exhibit buyer away in a heartbeat, as it surely does. Fortunately, this book will demonstrate how going green can reduce costs substantially while strengthening your company's reputation, and perhaps even helping to increase the value of its stock.[8]

The Green Double Edge

That's one half of what I mean by finding the "Green Edge." It's a competitive edge. It says that going green offers cost and brand performance advantages over the ways most organizations are currently handling their meetings, conferences, trade shows, product launches and other events. These tangible financial benefits are available to every meeting planner and exhibitor, and this book will show you how to gain access to them.

Perhaps you despair, though, because you've followed some popular advice and tried a few online carbon calculators, but have never found any of it particularly helpful when the time came to make specific choices. I'm afraid you've run into the other half of the "Green Edge." It's the half that acknowledges just how new going green still is. The Green Edge is the cutting edge, where innovations are popping up every year and new opportunities for competitive advantage are abundant, but where things haven't matured enough to provide answers to all of our questions. Well, cheer up: This book will guide you through this new and confusing green business landscape, and show you how to make sense of the issues in practical terms. That's where you'll find the Green Edge advantage.

This Book Is a Solution

In their 2006 bestseller *Green to Gold*, Daniel Esty and Andrew Winston identified what they called the "middle management squeeze":

> More than anywhere else in the organization, middle management is where the rubber meets the road in the drive for Eco-Advantage. The senior executive team hears the CEO's call for an environmental focus, and the line workers often welcome the chance to make their companies more eco-friendly. But middle managers are pulled in many directions. They face critical trade-offs and hard choices on a day-to-day basis. They're told to increase sales and throughput, cut costs, fatten profit margins—and now, be green as well.[9]

If this sounds like your predicament, you must be a meeting organizer, exhibit manager or an industry supplier. Let's be clear: The many voices that are urging you to go green—from senior executives to marketing colleagues, line workers, trade associations, outside stakeholders and activists, government regulators, the news media, investors and customers—cannot tell you exactly how to apply sustainability principles in your day-to-day job. Right? I think we can do better. Green leaders are proving that the supposed tension between business performance and environmental performance is just another busted myth. As you'll see, improving sustainability tends to create stronger brands with more loyal customers.

So how do we get there? The truth is, you can green your exhibition or meetings program without going back to school or hiring expensive consultants. The basic principles are actually quite simple. This book applies those tried and true principles to the choices exhibit and meetings professionals make every single day. The mantra for middle managers is not that you should add sustainability to your already overwhelming workload. It's much more elegant and effective than that! The Green Edge mantra is *Make Every Decision a Green Decision.™*

In other words, going green doesn't involve piling an entirely new set of issues and decisions into your already overloaded in-box. You'll gain much bigger advantages, and gain more easily, by applying green thinking to the decisions that you are already going to make today, tomorrow, next week, next month and so on. This guidebook will show you how to do that.

The solutions are simple, but implementing them will take some effort and creative thinking on your part too. This book distills the best available information about sustainability, and runs it through the filters of shop and show floor experience to deliver practical options. But your program is also unique. You'll need to apply these lessons in ways that fit your company's brand image and event schedule. Fortunately, in an industry that relies so heavily on teamwork, your core suppliers can help you implement many of the cost-effective green actions that are outlined in this book and quickly build momentum. So we'll dive into the challenge of motivating your team as well.

Finding the Green Edge

Why am I so confident this will work for you? It's because there is so much low-hanging fruit waiting to be picked. Consider a fairly common situation on the show floor.

Thousands of people descend on convention centers every week to deliver and unload exhibits, assemble them, plug in electric power, hang signs and overhead lights, tune multimedia programs, rehearse performances, troubleshoot conference audio-visual systems, roll out carpets, clean, remove waste, ensure security, serve meals and coordinate all of these activities. Many of these people, including you, probably arrive from out of town, so you're staying in hotels, eating in restaurants and utilizing a range of local transportation and entertainment services if you can spare a few hours to relax. More than anything else, a convention center hosts a community of busy people representing hundreds or even thousands of different companies and organizations. And every one of these people has a relatively good paying job, which means that their employers are paying taxes, supervising compliance with health and safety regulations, funding inventories, managing capital and paying interest to banks, compensating their suppliers, and, one hopes, turning profits.

Now that you have this image in your mind—the convention center as a beehive of activity in which each and every hour equates to money coming out of exhibitors', show organizers' and contractors' pockets—you can understand why everyone in the hall spends the set-up days tripping over scraps of lumber, packing foam, wrapping paper, bubble pack, shrink wrap, wads of tape, cardboard, banding and heaps of other discarded items that clog the aisles. It all comes down to a simple economic equation: Materials and energy are relatively cheap compared to the much higher cost of labor. When push comes to shove, it costs less to waste energy and materials than hours. So that's what we do. That's what everyone does.

Have you ever found yourself standing in your booth waiting for one or two last-minute graphics to arrive before your boss shows up? Your exhibit house says the graphics are on their way, and you've got the tracking number. But you haven't seen anything yet. It's getting late, and you're using various well-honed techniques to stay calm, so you won't gnaw your nails down to the quick.

When a forklift finally nestles its precious cargo onto your carpet, you feel a huge sense of relief. Your team unscrews the lid to reveal the fabulous marketing messages within. They apply a few strips of Velcro® and slap the graphics up on the walls (carefully, of course) or slip them into light boxes and voilá: Your booth is ready for showtime. And you are ready to welcome your boss into the company's brand presentation with confidence in a job well done.

But what about that wooden shipping box? It's out of sight and already out of mind. Chances are, your graphics will be going home with their cohorts in some other crate, so the box sitting on the edge of your carpet has completed its useful life. It was just a "one-way shipper." Your crew shoves it into the aisle and that's the last thought you or anyone else will ever give it. Its fate was sealed the moment it was conceived; its job now finished, it will be hauled away and crushed in a landfill.

Did you happen to notice what it was made of? It might have featured quality plywood, possibly even birch plywood, which is a furniture-grade material used to build exhibit walls and cabinets. If the box held several graphics mounted to heavy PVC panels, it might have been reinforced with lumber ribs and had 2" x 4" forklift skids on the bottom as well. Why did the shop use such expensive resources for a one-way shipper? That's easy: Labor costs more than materials. In the heat of the moment, expensive, long-lasting materials make for precise, reliable work that doesn't take very much time to complete. Using high-grade materials actually helped your shop control its labor costs when its crew fulfilled your last-minute request. Those materials performed admirably too. The shop folks knew that your one-way shipper was going to take some abuse, and less expensive cardboard would never have survived. But your all-important graphics did survive, and that, in a nutshell, was everyone's top priority.

This is how businesses view our natural resources and waste challenges today, and the meetings, events and exhibition industry is no different from most others. It's a simple matter of costs versus benefits. Businesses are very good at learning how to do expensive things more efficiently. High-cost processes get most of our attention, often to the detriment of other concerns. Now, however, organizations are beginning to realize that being wasteful has a price too. What did those last-minute graphics cost you anyway? Did you pay a 100 percent rush charge to have them printed overnight and an extra 50 percent in overtime labor to have them boxed and shipped? What did that one-way shipper really cost? What did you spend to have it flown to the local airport and then trucked in a hurry to the convention center? And what did the drayage company charge at their special handling rate to deliver it to your booth late at night? It wasn't cheap! You can add up the bills and decide whether that high-pressure, last-minute flurry of activity was worthwhile. That's basic management, and it's what exhibit professionals do every day.

Until recently, though, a different set of costs never made it into the exhibit manager's calculations. The environmental price—which in this case includes impacts on the forests, rivers and local communities where lumber is harvested to the health consequences of air pollution from shipping logs to mills for processing into plywood and then delivering the products to exhibit houses—does not appear on your invoices. Nor do the bills on your desk include line items for the consequences of carbon and toxic pollution that resulted from flying your graphics to the show. These environmental costs of doing business are what economists call "externalities," which is just a fancy way of saying they don't show up on your graphics and freight bills. We do pay for them, of course, but we pay in the form of taxes, healthcare premiums and in other ways that are not on our minds when we're making logistics decisions on the show floor.

Times are changing. Increasingly, businesses, regulators, non-governmental organizations, the news media and consumers are taking these external costs into account. If you are feeling pressure from upper management to go green, it's probably because they are feeling the heat themselves, either from outside forces or because they realize that big environmental changes put your markets, your company and its bottom line at risk. As we'll see, they are not alone.

Now, let's imagine a different scenario on the show floor. Suppose you call your exhibit house and tell them you've got a last-minute graphic coming their way. Your supplier swings into action on your behalf, just as they always have, but this time they receive the artwork electronically over the Internet. Then what? Your supplier contacts another company located near the convention center where you are standing. You and your exhibit house might be on opposite sides of the continent or the world, but your graphic arrives near you at the speed of light for next to no cost.

The nearby graphics house prints and mounts your graphic and wraps it in simple, inexpensive padding—possibly even a recycled material made from post-consumer waste—and then drives it over to the convention center. What does this flurry of activity cost? With electronic transfer you gained at least 24 hours, so you probably reduced the rush charges and you certainly eliminated an expensive shipping crate and a costly airfreight bill, not to mention all of the environmental and health costs associated with the crating and airfreight. Scenarios like this help illustrate where we can find our Green Edge.

Did you notice that we didn't have to rethink how our entire industry does business in order to make a big eco-friendly difference? My favorite analogy for finding the Green Edge is homey because it involves a towel that's sopping wet and dripping all over the bathroom floor. A towel is a tool. It's something you'll want to reuse, and you'd probably like it to dry out so that it's ready to go the next time you need it. But when it's saturated with so much water, it will stay soaking wet for a long time even if you hang it up on the clothesline. If, on the other hand, you wring the towel out before hanging it up, you'll be in business. The fabric will still be damp, but once the excess saturation is squeezed out, it can dry fairly quickly, even in an enclosed hotel bathroom. The big, happy secret about sustainability is that there's so much waste embedded in what we do in our work. The processes we use are practically dripping with excess energy that isn't really necessary. Wringing out that excess waste is easy and cost-effective to do. You might not be aware of the potential savings because most of the waste is out of sight and out of mind. So we take it for granted, and we're paying for it too.

That's the central image in the Green Edge approach to meetings and trade show programs, and it's our first Big Idea: *Just Wring Out the Waste.*

And let's be honest: You can't possibly eliminate every last little bit of environmental harm from these events anymore than we can wring a towel completely dry. That's just not possible. Nor is it the point because squeezing out a tremendous amount of waste isn't difficult and it leaves behind what we care about most, which is the opportunity to conduct effective face-to-face education, networking, sales and marketing.

As our energy systems and other technologies become more sustainable in the coming years and decades, this industry will benefit from those improvements too, just as a hand-wrung towel benefits from being hung on the line. And, as you'll see in the last chapters of this book, our industry might also find new ways to become more sustainable through innovative business models in the coming years. You don't have to get all the way there in one giant step. I doubt such a step would even be possible. But you can make a very significant difference right now, today, tomorrow, next week and next month, simply by learning how to eliminate the waste that you'd probably rather not pay for anyway.

This book asks two simple questions: How can exhibitors and their suppliers reduce the environmental consequences of their decisions while, at the same time, reducing their financial costs? And how can we achieve these goals without sacrificing the marketing and other face-to-face opportunities that our organizations are looking for in the first place? These are simple questions. I'll make the answers simple too.

Is This Book for You?

I wrote this book for exhibit, event and meetings managers because, as Esty and Winston put it, you are "where the rubber meets the road in the drive for Eco-Advantage." But share this information with your suppliers too. We work as teams in this industry, and the contents of this book will help your suppliers help you and your organization in its drive to achieve sustainability. I also wrote this book with the U.S. meetings industry in mind. But again, share its content globally as well. The insights and ideas are universal, even if they might be applied somewhat differently in other places around the world.

There is one other reason to focus on the industry in North America. A 2011 study by the Convention Industry Council titled, *The Economic Significance of Meetings to the U.S. Economy* "quantified the economic contributions of 1.8 million meetings, trade shows, conventions, congresses, incentive events and other meetings"[10] in the United States. About 10,700 of these events were trade shows, and the rest included business meetings, incentive meetings and other corporate and professional events. This research revealed that the industry supports an estimated 1.7 million jobs directly with $253 billion in spending. However, these numbers do not include all of the suppliers involved in the industry and their employees. Taken together, the so-called direct and indirect spending adds up to a total economic significance to the U.S. economy of more than $907 billion.[11] These are big numbers, and they suggest that the industry has a significant environmental footprint. They also suggest that if we wring our towels out we will make sizable contributions to the performance and welfare of our organizations, the economy, the public health and the world we leave to the next generations.

In many ways, you are in the driver seat. You make decisions that directly impact your organization's costs, brand image and the environment. You manage a supply chain that is designed to be creative and responsive, so your decisions can influence how they do business too. The authors of *Green to Gold* are exactly right: Meetings and event managers do their work where the rubber meets the road.

The Promise

A lot of business books present case studies that are fascinating to read about, yet difficult to apply. I get that. I also get that middle managers are way too busy to fill in the blanks between general principles and specific decisions. So this is not one of those business books. Instead, this book consolidates high-quality information from some of the most reputable sources and applies it directly to the questions and choices that you face all the time. In addition to addressing specific questions, however, the research for this book also revealed a few big ideas that can become your guiding principles as you work to embrace the promise of sustainability. I'll call these ideas out as we go along to make sure you see them clearly.

Meanwhile, this book recommends specific green actions that you can apply to reduce your costs and improve environmental performance right away. We'll keep it simple by providing enough context to help you decide whether the proposed actions fit your program, but not so much that you feel like you are back in school.

Who Is Making This Promise?

I've been creating and coordinating exhibition programs in this industry for 30 years. For 25 of those years I've owned and operated a creative services and project management agency, which has given me direct access to the executive leaders of Fortune 1000 corporations, as well as start-ups, in a wide range of industries. I've worked with the leadership of government agencies, science museums and public aquariums on many environmental communications projects as well. And I've been an exhibitor, which was an eye-opening experience because I suddenly understood the financial, brand image and scheduling pressures that managers feel firsthand. It is always helpful to take a walk down both sides of the street.

None of this makes me a research scientist or a journalist, for that matter. I am a communications expert and business owner with graduate school training in logic and social ethics. Perhaps because of this, I've spent one track of my career in creative marketing, and the other helping eminent scientists translate their research results into the language that the rest of us speak. This science translation work has taught me to be cautious about the claims people make when they cherry-pick data to support their green marketing claims. It's also taught me to respect a hierarchy of reliable scientific reporting, with broad assessments by esteemed scientific organizations at the top, individual peer-reviewed research papers in respected journals next, and finally the open marketplace of ideas where anything goes at the bottom. Above all, it's taught me to seek advice from technical experts when in doubt.

The suggestions in this book rely on some of the most respected data sources, and I've applied them according to the research community's cautions and caveats. I'll briefly explain why the caveats matter when they come into play, and this information will prove invaluable to you as you weigh the claims that marketing and sales people make about sustainability. I've been applying this research to our industry, in particular, since 2008, first out of a strong sense of personal commitment, and later as the author of the "Ask Mr. Green" sustainability blog at *ExhibitorOnline* and as the host of a podcast at ClimateReport.com. These experiences have opened the door to many of our colleagues from across the industry who generously share their expertise in their specific domains.

The attitude and optimism in this book are entirely my own. My firm has received its share of accolades for environmental leadership, and I have witnessed firsthand how improving environmental performance builds a company's momentum. That's how we became the first U.S. firm to receive "sustainable company" certification from FAMAB, the German exhibition industry's trade association. We were also the first marketing communications company to seek and receive certification under the

APEX/ASTM Environmentally Sustainable Meeting Standards. The certifications and various green awards have also introduced me to a host of other business professionals who embody the same can-do ingenuity that drives our work.

Bottom line: Going green works. I've lived it, and I've seen others prove it too. How could it be otherwise? We work in one of the most creative industries on earth. If we can't figure out how to operate more profitably and sustainably at the same time, then who can?

So let's get to it.

Chapter One

How to Use This Book

This is a how-to, not a who-done-it, so you don't have to read straight through from cover-to-cover to solve the mystery. If you are already well-versed in the business case for cost-effective green action, for example, and you're looking for advice about a specific issue, you might go straight to the chapter on exhibit materials, transportation, travel, literature and premiums, hospitality events and managing your supply chain. There you will find specific recommendations that will improve your program's eco-performance. The chapter on carbon metrics and its companion case study explain what you can measure and how to do it, and you'll discover how making a few simple calculations can reveal Green Edge opportunities that you might never have considered before.

Do you require sustainability certifications for meetings and events programs? A chapter on this topic explains the best options for this industry, and in the appendix you will find a table showing how the green actions suggested in this book address each of the categories that certification auditors will be looking for. And if you're wondering how to go public, report green achievements or market your organization as a sustainable brand, you'll find some sound advice in the certification chapter too.

Finally, if you want to think big about the future of the industry, and explore some ideas about doing business in new ways, you'll discover a few thought-provoking suggestions in the last chapters. If you do read straight through from start to finish, you will also see how a small number of big ideas pop up again and again, and build upon each other in surprisingly productive ways.

Green the Program, Not the Event

Make no mistake: This book is about taking big bites, not just nibbling at the edges. You are liable to discover how one green action leads to another, and it's the combinations of steps and their attendant benefits that generate the biggest savings and the corresponding environmental benefits. That's not to say that each and every eco-friendly action will yield a large financial return, but by concentrating on the substantial-looking opportunities, you'll discover how quickly the fiscal and environmental co-benefits can add up.

That's our approach: We're looking for larger opportunities to *Just Wring Out the Waste*, and we'll find them by applying the Green Edge mantra, *Make Every Decision a Green Decision,™* to the job you are already doing.

I realize that finding the Green Edge in your day-to-day work might not seem very exciting or even likely at first. If you pay much attention to news coverage of environmental issues, in fact, you might be expecting something quite different. The news emphasizes big, must-see, attention-getting stories, which can give you the erroneous impression that what the real-world work managers do behind the scenes to rack up eco-efficiencies is somehow unimportant.

A similar phenomenon can happen in the meetings industry, where exhibitors, not meeting managers, attract so much attention with new designs at major events. You can read, for example, about Heidelberg Druckmaschinen AG's dazzling exhibit and the company's impressive carbon emissions-cutting strategies at a show called Durpa 2012,[1] or Keen Inc.'s fashionable reuse of discarded shipping pallets in the design and construction of their exhibit booth for the 2010 Outdoor Retailer show.[2] We all love new projects and pretty pictures, and, after all, the exhibition hall is where so much of the hard work everyone is doing comes together. But don't let this lead you to think that the Green Edge is only waiting for you on the show floor. Pay equal attention to the work you do outside the limelight because that's exactly where so much of the meaningful action really takes place. And if your job involves managing conferences and meetings, rather than trade shows, this should come as good news.

Besides, reducing costs and improving environmental performance at a single event, whether it's a trade show or some other type of meeting, can be a real challenge. Even if your company earns headlines with an impressive new green exhibit at one show, what happens at the next show and the next one after that? How does the eco-progress you make carry over to the rest of your program? The fact that you manage a number of different events each year and that they share common resources and procedures is actually quite important and helpful. You already know something about spreading costs and savings across your annual schedule. The same ideas apply to going green. That's why you'll find it helpful to look at your entire program.

So keep the Green Edge mantra in mind to *Make Every Decision a Green Decision.*™ In other words, let's not treat sustainability as a separate task that you have to find extra time to accomplish somehow. We both know that won't work. Instead, let's find greener options within the work you're already going to do today, tomorrow, next week and beyond.

Suppose, for example, that you're not ready for a new booth quite yet. How can you use what you have more efficiently? Do you want to leave it alone or invest in one or two specific green upgrades? Do you know which upgrades would make the most sense? Or, let's say you do need to replace your booth right now. Do you want to build something new, rent something or rebuild your old properties into a fresh presentation? If you are going to build something new, which materials, processes and equipment will be more environmentally friendly? And, if you're considering a rebuild or a rental program, do you know how to maximize the tax advantages of your eco-choice?

Part of any purchase decision involves plans for shipping, crating, and routing from the shop to the show and back again. You'll want to consider the greenest and most cost-effective shipping package for your show schedule.

Does it pay to print and distribute brochures and product cut sheets? Do people think well of your company when they receive logo-emblazoned premiums? Are some giveaways greener than others?

If your company stages hospitality events or client dinners, do you know how to make greener decisions about food and how it is served?

And, of course, everyone on your team will be traveling to the meeting or the trade show, which means there are choices to be made about how they'll travel and where they'll stay.

The following chapters will tackle this long list of everyday decisions. The tendency, for all of us, will be to focus on just one question at a time, but it turns out that the easiest way to find your Green Edge is to look at the bigger picture. This leads us to the second Big Idea: *When In Doubt, Zoom Out.*

Zoom Out for a Better View

We sometimes find ourselves on the horns of dilemmas in which we can't seem to find any clear winners. Which choice is greener? Which is less expensive? Which is better? As vexing as these questions may seem, chances are you can't find the answers either because they don't exist or because the consequences of your decision would be rather small. Don't waste your time fretting about them. Just make a choice and move on. We have bigger fish to fry.

Zooming out brings more of your program into view, and it's the best way to find economies of scale. Here's a true story: The waste manager at a particular convention center was directed to slash the facility's landfill waste by three-quarters in just a few short years. She joked with me about how exhibitors would demand that she set up recycling stations for show badges. She was more than happy to comply, but if she could somehow capture every attendee's badge they would only fill a box or two. Her real challenge was all the packing materials, pallets, discarded cases of literature and abandoned booths that she had to cart away from the exhibit hall after every show. From her larger perspective, one or two boxes of show badges seemed trivial. She even mused that some of the people who pestered her about their badges might have been the folks who left half-empty cases of brochures in the aisles on their way out the door.

The challenge of getting the scale right is reminiscent of the story about plastic shopping bags. When British Prime Minister Gordon Brown embraced a nationwide ban on plastic bags to help fight global warming, the authors of *Sustainable Materials with Both Eyes Open* conducted an informal experiment. After a weekly trip to the supermarket, they put the groceries away and weighed the 13 empty plastic bags. The total was about 100 g, which is 0.22 lb. Then they weighed all of the plastic containers those 13 shopping bags had helped them carry home. Those containers, two-thirds of which were plastic bottles, weighed 10 times more than the bags: about 1 kg or 2.2 lb. In the United Kingdom, shopping bags account for less than one percent of the nation's total plastic consumption, and plastic causes about one percent of the nation's carbon emissions. So, banning plastic shopping bags would reduce national carbon emissions by less than 0.01 percent, which the authors claim is roughly equivalent to each person in the U.K. avoiding driving four miles per year.[3]

They were quick to point out other good reasons to eliminate plastic bags, not the least of which is the litter they cause. And in some developing economies, plastic shopping bags are valuable resources that serve many practical purposes. In the experiment, though, zooming out told the researchers that the shopping bag ban would make very little difference in solving a very large global problem.

Ironically, banning plastic bags might make an important contribution if it causes you, me and everyone else to cross a line in the sand that we are reluctant to cross. Getting someone to engage, take action and make a tangible commitment is a key ingredient in marketing and sales. It's one of the reasons why trade shows are worth their high costs: Face-to-face contact can help move people from passive observation to active purchasing. So there are two ways to look at green options that yield very small environmental benefits. The most useful way, by far, is to see that we have bigger fish to fry. When we can't split hairs with confidence, move on to more significant opportunities. The other way applies if and when we're having trouble taking that all-important first step and our colleagues and suppliers are balking too. In this instance, a small act that delivers a tangible reward might get us moving. If a small action will genuinely help us carry the bigger fish home and facilitate the more important changes we want to make, then it will have served a purpose.

It's a matter of keeping your perspective. Don't get stuck sorting the small fry or you'll spend all your time and energy chasing equally tiny benefits. Recycling show badges while throwing boxes of literature in the trash is a lost opportunity to save real money on printing, shipping and drayage, and reduce the environmental consequences of all that waste. More often than not, saving money and reducing eco-impacts go hand in hand, but you won't be able to see them unless you look at the bigger picture.

Zooming out can also help you prioritize green options that are a bit more expensive. Remember the shop owner who tells his clients that a green booth will cost 50 percent more than a standard booth? Many exhibitors stop right there and think they can't possibly afford to go green. Fifty percent sounds like a huge upgrade, especially when budgets are tight. Well, we can examine the validity of this claim by looking at the most common construction material in our industry—plywood—where the sustainable option sometimes actually does cost about 30 percent more than the standard material. How big a deal is the higher cost of sustainable plywood in the grand scheme of things?

Let's take a look. Roughly 60 percent of the price you pay for the new exhibit will go toward labor, and your choice of sustainable plywood won't change that figure at all. Plywood generally consumes one-quarter to one-half of the remaining budget. This portion of the budget will also be used to purchase carpet, acrylic, metals, high-pressure laminates, paint, graphics, lights and other equipment. If we split the difference right down the middle and say that plywood eats up 37.5 percent of our materials budget, then it only contributes 15 percent to the exhibit's total price: that's 37.5 percent (for plywood) of 40 percent (for all materials), in other words, 15 percent of the grand total. So if you choose sustainable plywood, your decision will only impact 15 percent of the total project. Sustainable plywood will add 30 percent to 15 percent, which is what the standard plywood already costs. Your green plywood upgrade therefore, adds just 4.5 percent to the total price of the exhibit.

$100,000 (total project) x 40% (for materials) =	$ 40,000
$ 40,000 (all materials) x 37.5% (for plywood) =	$ 15,000
$ 15,000 (plywood) x 30% (green upgrade) =	$ 4,500
$100,000 (total project) + $4,500 (green upgrade) =	$104,500

As the equations demonstrate, the percentages represent real dollars. But if the exhibit house had offered a 4.5 percent green plywood upgrade on your total price instead of a dire, 50 percent warning, you might have considered looking for ways to pay for it.

Let's take one more step, which involves amortizing the construction costs across multiple shows. Perhaps you plan to use the new exhibit three times each year for five years, which is a total of 15 events. Theoretically, you could spread the cost of the plywood upgrade over all 15 events, which would mean allocating an additional 0.3 percent of the build cost to each show. This sounds too good to be true and it probably is. Accountants might depreciate the purchase price over five years on the company's tax returns, but we're probably going to have to pay for the whole booth out of this year's budget. So, let's try amortizing the upgrade across this year's three events: that amounts to a 1.5 percent increase on the "build" line item per show. This cost sits next to other line items for booth space, sponsorships, multimedia programs, live presentations, transportation, travel, installation and dismantle labor, show services, hospitality, and much more.

Can you afford this? Will anyone notice that this line item increased by 1.5 percent, or that the total build price jumped 4.5 percent? It depends, in part at least, on how the company shares or compartmentalizes your budgets. Fortunately, we have a green strategy for either situation. Let's take a look.

If they compartmentalize, you'll have to find all of the savings within the construction budget itself. Fortunately, you're dealing with a custom-design project, not an off-the-shelf product, so we've got tremendous flexibility. We've already zoomed back from the plywood itself to the entire build, and this opened the door to something builders often call "value engineering." It's a process every designer and builder is familiar with. When a proposed design costs more than the exhibitor's budget, the team goes to work making refinements that will bring the costs in line without sacrificing the creative essence. Designers ask: Is there a design detail we can live without? Can we pick less expensive furnishings or equipment to make up the difference? Can we reuse some crates or other components that your company already owns? Exhibit houses solve riddles like these every day of the week, and while 4.5 percent isn't zero, it isn't an especially challenging number.

Leaving the construction budget behind for a moment, we can zoom out even further to explore how you allocate dollars across an entire show or a season's worth of shows. This gives us a much larger pool of numbers to work with, and as you already know, it opens the door to finding lots of ways to save money. What happens to that 4.5 percent green upgrade charge when you look at construction, media production, transportation, travel, literature, premiums, storage, hospitality, on-site staffing, press events and several other line items? Exhibit managers wrestle with these allocations all the time, too, and finding ways to save 4.5 percent of our new build cost by reprioritizing across multiple line items is nothing special.

Can you find enough savings to pay for this sustainability upgrade? Of course you can if it's a high priority. And if you embrace sustainability more fully, you will find even bigger opportunities to reduce costs than we've considered so far. *When in Doubt, Zoom Out.*

In the end, meeting the sustainability challenge has very little to do with affordability. It really has to do with whether buying sustainable plywood is the best way to wring out your particular towel. As you'll see throughout this book, it pays to prioritize.

And that means we need to get our priorities straight.

Chapter Two

How Green Is Green?

Yvon Chouinard, the founder of the iconic outdoor clothing company Patagonia, Inc., was once compared to another design-driven innovator, Apple's Steve Jobs.

> Interviewer: "Do you feel any connection and kinship between Patagonia and Apple?"
>
> Chouinard: "No, not at all. . . . You know, try and open up an iPhone and get it repaired. It's a disposable item. . . . 'Cause they don't want you to fix that iPhone, they want you to buy a new one next year. I can't relate to a company like that."[1]

Do Chouinard's views seem a little quirky to you or even extreme? To many people, sustainability looks like a utopian dream promoted by tree huggers, radical environmentalists and a few well-crafted consumer marketing campaigns. Patagonia, for example, which makes technical outdoor clothing from organic cotton and recycled soda bottles and is accredited by the Fair Labor Association,[2] says, "use business to inspire and implement solutions to the environmental crisis."[3] Chouinard's own essay on corporate social responsibility (CSR) features a five-step program: Lead an examined life, clean up your act, do your penance, support civil democracy and influence other companies.[4] It reads like a personal credo, as well as a vision statement that defines a brand.

One could even be cynical about it: Patagonia's products are designed for outdoor recreation, and their customer base includes more than its share of environmentalists. We tend to assume that leaders in such markets embrace sustainability through and through. With companies like Patagonia, Clif Bar and other eco-focused brands, we expect transparent management of their environmental footprints, fair treatment of employees and contractors, support for the communities they work in, and innovative and healthful products.

Well, guess what: going green is going mainstream. Wall Street likes to see it too:

> Using voluntary disclosures made through the CSR newswire service, we find that managers' disclosure decisions involving greenhouse gas emissions produce positive returns to shareholders. . . . For small companies in a limited public information environment, we find that mean adjusted share price increases significantly by 2.32 percent . . . around the CSR newswire release date. Our sample of disclosing companies received an aggregate market value boost from their CSR newswire releases of approximately 10 billion dollars, independent of differences in public information availability.[5]

In other words, the companies' stock prices rose just because they published their greenhouse gas emissions data. And the companies who got the boost were by no means tree-hugger brands. Unlike Patagonia and Clif Bar, which are privately owned, the 10-billion-dollar stock boost went to 84 publically traded, U.S.-based corporations in markets ranging from consumer goods to energy, financials, health care, industrial products, information technology, materials, telecommunications and utilities. Perhaps your company was even on the list.

Investors place genuine value on climate-change reporting. Companies that take environmental responsibility seriously are literally worth more than those that don't. So green is going mainstream and spilling over from marketing departments into business operations. Your work on meeting and event programs straddles these two worlds, where the company's image and reputation meet practical, cost-conscious management decisions every day.

Is your company talking the sustainability talk? A quick tour of corporate websites shows that sustainability statements are popping up like weeds. Check out companies as diverse as Apple, Coca-Cola, Deloitte, General Electric, Ikea, 3M, Charles Schwab and SMG: They all present environmental policies and progress reports online. As GreenBiz.com notes, "Most companies now disclose at least some environmental impacts, and a growing number are having third-party assurance completed on their quantified performance data to make their reporting more credible."[6]

Something is clearly going on here, but what is it?

The answer seems to be threefold. The first part involves stakeholder expectations: customers, regulators, employees and others including non-governmental organizations (NGOs) are demanding higher standards of corporate conduct. Gone are the days when a company's CSR policy can consist of simply contributing a few nature programs on public television while it continues doing business as usual. In the age of cell phone cameras and social media, everyone is a potential source of information about a company's real behavior, and public disclosures can pack a wallop.

In a now-famous case study, Greenpeace targeted Nestlè's Kit Kat brand with a campaign on YouTube.[7] Kit Kat was buying palm oil from an Indonesian supplier that was engaged in widespread deforestation and destruction of orangutan habitat. Nestlè countered that it only used a tiny fraction of global palm oil production (0.7 percent), but the social media campaign went viral. The company eventually changed suppliers, held meetings with Greenpeace to disclose its palm oil sources, partnered with another NGO called Forest Trust to certify the sustainability of its palm oil purchases, and eventually joined the Roundtable for Sustainable Palm Oil, a broad partnership seeking to end unsustainable production.[8] Nestlè's experience shows how powerful these unexpected disclosures can be. People are watching corporate behavior on many fronts, including child labor (Nike), conditions in overseas factories (Apple), toxic pollution (Erin Brockovich and Pacific Gas & Electric) and more. The ubiquitous availability of video cameras and social media raises the stakes, and it's a core principle of corporate survival to be for what's happening in society at large. Today CSR and sustainability are happening.

Kit Kat shows how important sustainability has become to brand reputations. You see companies awakening to this new reality on the show floor as well. For example, in 2008 Hewlett Packard worked to build a greener exhibit booth because, according to design manager Milena Pastori, "HP wanted not just its products but also its booth to prove how it can impact the environment in a friendly way."[9] A few years later, the German printing press manufacturer Heidelberg Druckmaschinen AG recognized that its trade show program was not living up to the company's 20-year-long commitment to improving environmental performance. As a result, the company targeted the show floor as a place to make sweeping changes and bring its brand image and corporate values into alignment.[10] These companies recognize that, when it comes to sustainability and corporate social responsibility trade shows and meetings can't be considered "behind the scenes" any longer.

The second answer is that the value of going green runs deeper too: It goes directly to the bottom line. In one analysis after another, global demand for energy and raw materials is clearly rising, and smart companies are taking steps to reduce their exposure to volatile prices. *The State of Green Business 2014* report from GreenBiz.com notes that companies in very diverse markets are "recognizing that elevating sustainability leads to innovations, efficiencies and improved resilience amid turbulent markets . . . ."[11] In simple, practical terms, energy and resources are becoming more expensive, and going green is a smart way to save money.

The third answer is actually embedded in the second: Smart companies are beginning to take the elevated risks of extreme weather, damage to facilities, interruptions of supply lines, weakened employee health and lost productivity quite seriously. The word "resilience" is all the rage among environmentalists, governments, scientists and business leaders these days. Perhaps we should ask, "Resilience in the face of what, exactly?"

Tomorrow Won't Be Like Yesterday

A brief tale might be helpful. One night, when my father was an infant, he was fussing away in his crib below an open window. Responding as any parent does, my grandmother went to see what the commotion was all about. After settling him down she stood up and found herself staring into the eyes of a black panther. Luckily for me, the story had a happy ending!

This tale originated on a summer evening in 1932, somewhere in the hills above an Indian town called Saharanpur. In those days, India's entire population was about 290 million people, plus quite a few large cats. That's nearly the population of the United States today, which is approaching 320 million.[12] Coincidentally, it was also around 1930 when the global population reached 2 billion for the first time in history. And at those numbers, I'm told you could still drive your Model-A Ford around a curve in India and find a tiger sitting by the roadside. Not anymore. Population growth is exponential, and in 2011 the world reached a new milestone: 7 billion people. India's population has more than quadrupled since 1932 and is now above 1.2 billion. And not so far away, China is home to an additional 1.4 billion people.

This is where things get interesting: The population of the United States, Canada, the European Union, Australia, New Zealand and Japan combined, which is an admittedly inadequate snapshot of the industrialized world, is significantly less than half the population of India and China. This comparison ignores many other countries, but even so it presents a startling picture: The number of people in this world who enjoy the greatest wealth and development is overwhelmed by the number who are now coming into their own, and who have aspirations for continued economic growth and Western-style consumerism.

Where does this leave us? One thing is certain: In the coming years, we'll face much greater competition for the resources our industry uses most—wood, steel, aluminum, plastic, textiles and fuel. The International Energy Agency and other analysts, for example, think that demand for steel will increase 150 percent and aluminum consumption will jump 250 percent by 2050.[13] With numbers like these, it's easy to see why price volatility is a growing concern for every business. It's simply good business practice to learn to conserve resources and save money sooner rather than later.

Beyond this, however, the sheer pressures of population, development and pollution are changing the game in unexpected ways. I interviewed *Earth: The Operators' Manual* author and National Academy of Sciences member Richard Alley on the *Climate Report™* podcast about the growing potential for abrupt, unexpected changes.[14] He observed, among other things, that the boundaries separating the wet and dry regions of the world are fairly sharp, and they are migrating toward the poles. If you happen to live near one of these boundaries, you might suddenly find yourself on the other side as it passes by, where conditions will be dramatically different.

If the shifting line happens to cross a national border, you could become a climate refugee. If not, your business and livelihood might still be altered forever.

To explore this, I spoke with a researcher about how this very change is affecting the wine industry.[15] The prospects are not very promising: The evidence suggests that in the world's major wine producing regions, the areas that are suitable for growing grapes will decrease between 25 percent and 75 percent before the year 2050.[16] California winemaker Steve Matthiasson responded that this breathtaking shift is happening faster than farmers can pay the 40-year mortgages on their vineyards. So while some of the larger corporate winemakers are busy buying land farther north and at higher elevations, the unprecedented transformation of their industry's most basic resources—land, weather and water—puts smaller companies at greater risk. And as Matthiasson observed, it also raises questions about the future of their product quality and brand reputations in a rather finicky market. Matthiasson wasn't kidding when he said that when the weather becomes less predictable, growers are literally betting the farm.

The CEO of a major food products company agreed when he told me privately that he now requires each of the company's directors, including the marketing and trade show staff, to develop plans to reduce carbon pollution because, as he put it, they are farmers. If the climate changes they might be out of business.

But if these stories strike you as far-fetched or way beyond the scope of your job, you're not alone! A National Research Council's (NRC) report about the practical side of global environmental change opens with an astounding statement: "Government agencies, private organizations, and individuals whose futures will be affected by climate change are unprepared, both conceptually and practically, for meeting the challenges and opportunities it presents."[17] In other words, none of us is accustomed to what's in store, and we haven't figured out how to plan for it yet. The NRC continues: "Many of [our] usual practices and decision rules . . . assume a stationary climate—a continuation of past climatic conditions. . . . That assumption, fundamental to the ways people and organizations make their choices, is no longer valid."[18]

So we are entering an era when businesses will face unprecedented competition for resources and increasingly volatile prices, plus the prospects of very large environmental changes. As we've seen, investors are taking this seriously, and they are rewarding companies that are willing to confront the future and rethink their plans. The word "resilience" is right on the money. Customers, too, are beginning to expect businesses to respond to the changing world, and green leaders from many different industries are recognizing that their brand reputations can be strengthened or weakened by the choices they make on the trade show floor.

If you happen to work for a company like Patagonia, Clif Bar, Interface or one of the other eco-focused brands, perhaps you've been asked to make your meetings or trade show program more sustainable, so that it will reflect the company's values. As Patagonia says, "use business to inspire and implement solutions to the environmental crisis." Have you been asked to make your solutions big? The State of California made that type of move in 2006 by setting an 80-percent reduction target for statewide greenhouse gas emissions over about 40 years. California took this bold step because the scientific evidence shows that it's the best way to avoid crossing the threshold that world leaders consider dangerous.[19] Perhaps your company wants you to do something equally bold. Alternatively, your green mandate might be focused elsewhere, such as buying whatever you can from local sources in order to support the communities we work in. Or you might be targeting a few, very specific resources or forms of pollution that reflect your company's top priorities.

On the other hand, if your company is new to sustainability, or is looking to avoid trouble with regulators, customers and NGOs, your mandate might not be bold at all. If so, you are not alone. Even though more and more businesses are embracing sustainability, GreenBiz.com reports that, ". . . progress remains incremental and slow. The scale, speed and scope of change appear to be inadequate to the challenges we face."[20] Andrew Winston, coauthor of the business bestseller, *Green to Gold*, said much the same thing in a fascinating discussion about corporate sustainability on the *Climate Report.*™ [21]

Why do we find such a wide range of views? As the NRC pointed out, very few people have really come to terms with what the future might be like, and business leaders are no exception. So your mandate might or might not be far reaching. In this new age of transparency, time will tell whether consumers, activists and other stakeholders will eventually force companies to take bigger, bolder steps. Perhaps they will. For the time being, though, one thing is clear: Taking sustainability seriously increases shareholder value, protects brand reputations, saves money and prepares a business for whatever might come its way.

Where does this leave you? You're probably wondering how, in your role as an exhibit manager, you are supposed to cope with these global challenges. The answer is not very different from the ways in which you cope with every other challenge in your events program. When something doesn't show up on show site, a crucial piece of equipment breaks down, the featured graphic is defaced, or a cabinet gets crushed in shipment, what do you do? You look at the problem in light of your priorities, figure out what steps need to be taken and get busy. Our industry can't possibly solve global environmental problems alone, nor is that really your job. But we do have an important role to play in making our companies more competitive, our industry more sustainable and our world more resilient.

This means it's time to use our problem-solving skills and insights to figure out how to find the Green Edge.

Chapter Three

How to Go Green

When it's time to do something challenging, where do you start? You could stick your toe in the water, see how it feels and then slowly ease yourself in. You could decide to focus on just one thing at a time, maybe building a greener booth before tackling other issues. You could set a modest goal, along with some incremental stages, such as trying to reduce show floor waste five percent each year for five years. You could even skip setting goals altogether and just make a checklist of green actions that you'd like to take. You could. Everything would seem perfectly reasonable.

The trouble is that the companies that are having real success finding the Green Edge don't start that way. Companies like Johnson & Johnson, 3M, Nike, Proctor & Gamble, Starbucks, Intel, Toyota and many others take a different approach. They dive right into the deep water and start swimming. More often than not, they decide to go for the impossible right away by setting "stretch goals," a term coined by the bestselling authors of *Green to Gold*: "Stretch goals drive creativity by asking the near impossible and demanding the reexamination of assumptions. They force everyone to search for new ways to meet old goals." [1]

The most successful green business programs are not built upon baby steps, yet the companies that use stretch goals fully expect to achieve them: "We're focusing . . . on big advances that present a challenge and might seem nearly impossible. The stretch goals we've seen animating corporate culture give life to the mindset principle 'No is not an option.'"[2]

Nothing is tentative about this approach, nor is it vague. The lofty goals set by winning green performers aren't just pie-in-the-sky daydreams. The most effective stretch goals are ambitious and far reaching, yet the targets are also clear and specific. DuPont's "the goal is zero" waste-reduction campaign, for example, sounds almost too ambitious to mean anything at all, but as the authors point out, "zero" is a specific number and it's easy to visualize. The clarity that comes from the number "zero," impossible looking though it may be, brings focus to the green initiative and sets expectations for a very high level of performance. Other companies' winning stretch goals might be a little more concrete, yet they still seem nearly impossible to achieve. For example, Nike and 3M targeted reducing volatile organic compounds (VOCs) by 90 percent, a stretch goal that both companies achieved.[3]

It's quite unlikely that these companies would have gotten as far as they did had they chosen the cautious stick-your-toe-in-the-water approach instead of jumping in with both feet. Setting tentative goals is like telling your team that you're not really serious. What do people do when they're given a small challenge? They put it off until later. When you're on a tight show schedule, something else always seems to be more urgent, and everyone takes care of urgent priorities first. Reduce waste by five percent? "Sure, but later, right? What about getting these service orders in before the discount expires, sending these graphics files to the exhibit house ahead of the rush charge deadline, and coordinating these product shipments before the truck leaves and we have to use airfreight? These things need attention right now!"

The biggest problem with goals that don't feel urgent is that some other new priority always seems to come along and displace them. A friend once told me, "'Yes' means yes, 'no' means no and 'maybe' means no." "Later" tends to mean never. Worse yet, small objectives seem like somebody else's problem, not yours or mine. Who, after all, is supposed to take ownership of show floor waste anyway when you have so many other important things to do?

Remember that very expensive, high-quality, one-way graphic shipper? We already considered one reason why the shop built it: materials cost less than labor. But there's another reason too: neither you, nor your suppliers, can afford to fail. This is show business, after all, and none of us can imagine pitching prospective customers with a presentation that says we let the company down. So you, and just about every supplier you know, rely on habits that you can trust. When a crisis hits, you go with what you know, and those little toe-in-the-water green goals get kicked to the curb every time.

It's human nature, and it's what you're up against. Habits and consumption patterns are not just random; they embody years and years of reliable performance. They're costly, but they always work. When you decide to go green you're trying to redirect all of that momentum in a new direction. You'll never get there with a tentative nudge. Nike, Ford, Patagonia and the rest of them know that if you want to turn toward sustainability you're going to have to shock the system. Stretch goals do this, and the companies that insist on achieving the near impossible usually succeed. The bottom line is that stretch goals work.

My company tried stretch goals, too, by setting impossible sounding targets for reducing greenhouse gas emissions, water use, energy consumption and landfill waste in our office. When I presented the goals to our staff, one of them literally asked, "Are you crazy?" Perhaps I am, but with such stringent targets to meet, everyone began looking for ways to be more environmentally efficient. And within just 15 months we had cut our carbon emissions by 65 percent, gasoline 63 percent, employee driving and landfill waste 45 percent each, electricity by one-quarter and water by one-fifth.

When you set green goals, don't be shy. Demanding the near impossible works, as long as your goals are clear and specific. Consider these crazy-sounding goals, for example:

- Cut greenhouse gases from construction, transportation and travel by 50 percent within three years
- Build nothing new for the next seven years
- Reduce landfill waste by 90 percent next year
- Reduce shipping by 90 percent to next year's shows

These are just a few ideas to get you thinking in the right direction. Notice that each of these goals has a very challenging, but specific target and a deadline. Each is clear. Each focuses your attention on a definitive number. Each can be measured. Best of all, you're probably scratching your head and wondering, "Are you crazy? How could we possibly do that?" That's key: The purpose of stretch goals is to inspire creative thinking about doing something tangible. Stretch goals turn vague aspirations about environmental performance into concrete targets that people can take action to achieve.

So here is the next Big Idea: *Be Bold. Do the Impossible.*

It works. Just ask some of the nation's leading corporations. But remember that we're not throwing the baby out with the bathwater here. The unwritten rule in each and every stretch goal is that you must achieve it while still doing excellent marketing, sales, education or whatever it is that your events are supposed to be doing. The big innovation is that stretch goals will get you thinking about why you're doing events in the first place. What are you really trying to achieve? We all get sucked into the high-pressure routine of coordinating event after event, and some days we just go through the motions. Nothing is less environmentally efficient than spending a lot of time, energy and money just to follow a routine. When you challenge your team with goals that seem nearly impossible to achieve they'll quickly realize that you're asking something very basic: "Why are we doing this in the first place?"

There is no better starting point for event planning than this question. We often ask our clients, "Why are you attending that show? Why don't you skip it? Tell me why it's worth the money." We're not really suggesting that they should drop out. We're really asking them to identify the business opportunities that make investing in the event worth the money. If you can answer that question, then you can dial in your priorities and allocate resources to achieve them. You can also let the unimportant things go, and this is where managers sometimes discover financial savings and other resources that they never knew they had. Stretch goals make you confront these types of questions, along with a host of others: Do you really need a new booth yet? What do you gain by shipping something as opposed to renting something locally? Are all of your booth staffers delivering high value on show site or would their time be better spent back at the office? Is anybody following up on the show leads? Answering such questions will tell you where you can begin wringing out the towel right away without doing any harm to the company's prospects.

Fire Up the Team

But this doesn't mean pursuing your stretch goals will be easy. In fact, breaking career-long habits is difficult, and that's why teamwork is so important. Our staff called me crazy when I pitched the company's stretch goals. That was OK, I just kept asking questions: "Is there a more energy-efficient way to do this? Can we choose a greener product that still meets our performance requirements? Can we afford something even more efficient next time?" These questions quickly became ingrained in our thinking from top to bottom, and it wasn't long before the results began speaking for themselves. Once that started happening, we had momentum.

THE TIME IS NOW

On the day when the government of California decided to reduce statewide greenhouse gas emissions 80 percent by 2050, they were looking ahead roughly 45 years. A time horizon that long puts the goal line far enough away that it lets organizations get value out of the capital investments they've already made and plan ahead for major new spending. But when I thought about reducing our company's carbon emissions, it occurred to me that a design and management office doesn't own any long-lived capital equipment. Sure, our office has an air conditioner, and small businesses own company cars, but as Yvon Chouinard observed, the electronic equipment we own and lease goes out of date every few years and we replace it. Therefore, I reasoned that we wouldn't need to spend 45 years to achieve the state's emissions reduction target. Anything we might be able to accomplish 10 years from now we ought to be able to do just as easily within a year or two. So in picking a stretch goal, I decided to compress California's 45 year timeframe into just 12 years. Our near impossible stretch goal was to reduce the company's greenhouse gas emissions 80 percent by the year 2020. Sure enough, we got most of the way there within just 15 months.[4] Talk about wringing out the waste! That's almost overnight.

Think about the long-lived investments in your events program versus those things that you might be able to change almost immediately. If you own an exhibit, your company is probably depreciating its value over five years, and the properties themselves were probably built to last two or three times that long. This suggests that building a new green booth might not be your first and most productive order of business. You might be able to get the ball rolling and generate some momentum more quickly by focusing on other aspects of your program right away. For example, video displays and computers are often replaced after just two or three years, and newer models tend to get more energy efficient all the time, which makes them easy targets for improvement. Most companies reserve booth space a year in advance, so your booth sizes and floor plan shapes might be locked in for roughly one more season, but it's never too early to begin planning to do things differently by the time you renew your reservations. Budgets, too, are usually negotiated annually, so thinking about making rapid progress on a one-to-two year time horizon makes a lot of sense. Some graphics have long lives, but relatively few last longer than a year. Many get updated for each and every event, so there is no reason to put off looking for greener graphics production options. Just about everything else that you manage, from literature and giveaways, to transportation, rentals, hotels, hospitality events and booth staffing happens more or less on the fly. You can start making greener choices right now. There is no reason to wait.

These facts are telling you something very important: You don't have to wring the towel out slowly. We can give it a good squeeze right now, enjoy the benefits within a few months, get some more benefits next year, and build up momentum. Meanwhile, we can begin planning ahead for anything that requires a larger investment. *Being bold also means being quick.*

EXPOSE YOURSELF TO GET THE BALL ROLLING

Whether you receive your goals from senior management, come up with them on your own, or brainstorm with your coworkers, your first job is to write them down and present them to your entire internal and external team. Your mission is to make clear that your goals are not negotiable, and that you have no intention of failing. The team's mission, therefore, is to find ways to achieve your green stretch goals while still doing brilliant event marketing, sales, education, or whatever the case may be. It's their job to help you rethink everything from the ground up.

If you don't go public, you will almost certainly fail. And if you only go public to one team member at a time, they might have a hard time taking you seriously. Keep in mind that your suppliers might not know how to find the Green Edge on day one. This is where group dynamics can help you. A team-wide meeting to learn a client's goals for the coming years is a very big deal to the supplier team because it signals just how serious you are about your mission and your intentions to achieve it with their help. But beyond making a bold statement, it also sets the stage in a very practical way because environmental efficiency depends heavily on teamwork. Your shipping strategy, for example, involves how you will route shipments, whether you'll build crates, what you'll source locally versus ship long distance, and possibly how you will contend with last-minute requests from your colleagues. You can't do all of this with just one party at the table. You need your coworkers, the exhibit house, shipping company, installation contractor, and possibly others to join in the group effort. The great thing about having everyone at the table for a frank and honest discussion about your green goals is that members of your team will begin signaling to each other that they're ready to go. None of your suppliers wants to be left behind, and that competitive spirit will start the ball rolling. It's a great way to begin building momentum the right way. As is so often the case in business, the opposite is also true: It will be very, very difficult to make progress if you don't have the right people in the room.

Deciding to go green is a lot like deciding to go to the gym. It's easy to make the decision to join, but health clubs make most of their money on up-front initiation fees because so many people essentially drop out. It's hard to stick with the program alone. That's why so many coaches and fitness trainers encourage you to sign up for a class, join a team or agree to meet a workout partner at a specific time and place. On the days when you feel like blowing it off, you'll know that your "accountability buddy" is waiting for you. Green teams work the same way. When everyone knows you mean business, they will share the same expectations.

In fact, teamwork is so important to your overall success that it is the next Big Idea: *Go Public. Let Teamwork Pull You Forward.*

BE WILLING TO LEARN

Once you've made your stretch goals clear, you still need to participate in the process of brainstorming and problem solving. This is the role I played when I kept asking questions about energy efficiency in our office. I didn't know all the answers when we started, but I reminded everyone to find solutions that supported our top priorities. You're not expected to know all the answers either, but you will need to be the project champion so that your green goals take root and start to grow.

This is really the heart of the matter, and if you want the benefits of finding the Green Edge, you need to make sustainability a co-top priority with your number-one marketing, sales or educational objective. I often tell our clients that they can only have one top priority because, when push inevitably comes to shove, something always wins the day and everything else falls by the wayside. So how can you have co-top priorities when you're trying to mesh business with sustainability? Think of it this way: Your number one business performance goal, whether it's about marketing, sales or education, is just as important as it always was. The Green Edge difference is in how you go about achieving it. Sustainability is about committing yourself, and your team, to the greenest ways of achieving your top business objective. It's what the Green Edge mantra means in practical terms. If you *Make Every Decision a Green Decision,™* you'll still be managing the same program you've always managed and chasing the same performance goal that you've always chased, but you and your team will conduct the chase in much more sustainable ways. From this perspective, green goals and business goals are never in conflict at all.

But going green will be something new, and it might seem a little bit disruptive at first. Someone needs to be the project champion because your stretch goals will push everyone outside their comfort zones. When people feel pressured by everyday circumstance, their instincts will be to revert to the habits they already trust. Your questions and suggestions will be reminders that help prevent this from happening.

Give it some time. As part of our company's green business plan, we decided to slash the amount of driving employees were doing. We settled on two tactics that we thought might work, even though we expected them to cause some discomfort and disruption for a while. One was to give everyone a computer to allow telecommuting. We had no idea how this would work out because creative teams are a bit like rock bands: They feed off the group energy and shared creativity. We were concerned that letting people work in isolation might cause problems. But those who were commuting long distances were also pumping a lot of CO_2 into the air and exhausting themselves in the process, so we decided to give it a try.

Whenever we got frustrated, we reminded one another that we were conducting an experiment.

Our second move was to break a habit that we really trusted. Since we are consultants, designers and project managers, we meet with our fabrication partners often to turn over designs, review budgets, answer questions, perform quality assurance and help solve construction conundrums. Our familiar, reliable, well-worn habit involved having the leader of each project visit the shops as often as necessary to keep everything rolling smoothly. Our staff would drive to the office, then drive to a fabricator's shop for a meeting, then drive back to the office and then drive home at the end of the day. This used to be normal because, frankly, it worked so well. But when we looked at our stretch goal for carbon emissions, this trustworthy and familiar pattern suddenly looked like a terrible waste of time and gasoline, so we decided not to do this anymore. Our experiment was to assign almost all of the shop visits to the people whose commuting routes took them closest to the fabricators' facilities, and schedule virtually all of the meetings at the beginning or end of the workday. This meant project leaders would have to learn new ways to communicate with each other about their objectives and concerns because if a project leader didn't happen to live along a shop-commute route he or she wouldn't be visiting the fabricator very often anymore. Our hope was that all of the hours people wouldn't have to spend driving around would free them up to do more creative and productive work with a lot less stress. In other words, the stretch goal led us to rethink a proven system and hunt for a better alternative.

It took about a year for everyone to feel comfortable with these new schemes. But eventually we got used to them. Now those who live close to the office show up almost every day, but those who live very far away rarely come in more than once a week. Why did it take so long for everybody to adjust? When procedures change, people have to learn what they can expect from one another all over again, and it takes time for them to work the kinks out among themselves. As they experiment, though, they start falling into new grooves, and the new habits gradually become second nature, just as the old habits were. It's smooth sailing in our office today, but only because we treated the transition like an experiment and we were willing to listen, learn and adjust.

You'll be in a similar position with your internal stakeholders and your supplier team. Nobody will feel entirely comfortable at first. People might warn you that you're "taking awfully big risks." Just ask them whether they intend to fail? Are they going drop the ball? Of course not! In this business, nobody accepts failure, so a good way to handle the discomfort they're feeling might be to ask, "What can we do to minimize these risks without sacrificing our company's green goals?" Asking this question turns a vague sense of unease into a concrete, problem-solving exercise that will build confidence.

Your stretch goals will challenge expectations, and make people a little uncomfortable for a while. You'll want to create a spirit of experimentation, teamwork and mutual support to help people grow confident in a spirit of innovation. And don't worry, they will.

CAN THE DROPS FILL THE BUCKET?

In his book *Sustainable Energy: Without Hot Air*, David MacKay revisits the recycle-our-show-badges issue in a slightly different and even more pessimistic way. He says "doing one's bit" by unplugging your mobile phone charger saves exactly as much energy in a single day as driving an average car for one second. If you do it every day of the year you'll save as much energy as you spend taking one hot bath. That sure sounds discouraging. MacKay does urge you to unplug your charger, but not to be duped into thinking "every little bit helps." Instead, he says, "If everyone does a little, we'll achieve only a little."[5]

David MacKay might agree that stretch goals make much more sense. The thing is, if you are using stretch goals, you're not thinking about doing just one little thing; you're thinking about giving that wet towel a good, hard wringing out. So, while you don't want to be duped into thinking that each tiny action is more than a gesture, be sure to look at the other side of the coin too. Don't be discouraged by naysayers who focus on how insignificant each gesture is. Instead, ask yourself whether your plans are limited to taking a few baby steps.

Southern California Edison, a large electric utility company that's heavily invested in promoting energy efficiency, cites a U.S. Department of Energy statistic about turning things off. The DOE estimates that the average household wastes up to 20 percent of its electricity costs by leaving things—lots of things, not just mobile phone chargers—plugged in.[6] In other words, turning *every single one of our power strips off* at the end of the day, so that power isn't flowing to anything at all, can make a big difference. Since you pay for electrical outlets on the show floor, not the electricity you actually use, turning everything off in your booth at the end of each day won't put cash back in your pocket, but it is a sensible part of a comprehensive green action program.

DON'T LET THE QUEST FOR PERFECTION SLOW YOU DOWN

As you'll see in the next few chapters, green choices are not always as clear-cut as you might want them to be. Be prepared to accept tradeoffs and take incremental steps. It's perfectly reasonable, even essential, to do so in order to keep improving your performance.

If you're measuring and reducing carbon emissions, for example, and a group of executives suddenly decides to fly in for a show, your progress report might show a setback. Don't worry about a one-time blip. Business dishes up all sorts of unexpected requirements and compromises, and if you dwell on them, you might lose momentum. Suppose you spend two years planning to build a much, much greener booth in a location that will also reduce your shipping pollution to and from shows. At the last minute, you get blindsided by a budget cut and a requirement to go with a supplier in a different city. As you already know, compromises and tradeoffs are more the norm than the exception in this game. You live with them every day, and the process of going green will be no exception.

Take what you can get and move on. Doing so is entirely consistent with the "no is not an option" mentality behind stretch goals. As long as you keep moving, incremental progress is still progress, so look ahead to the long view. The things you have to compromise about today might be non issues down the road. And if you keep racking up environmental efficiencies as you go along, you're likely to be surprised by how much progress you actually make. Here's a great story: Executives at Alcan set a goal of reducing greenhouse gas emissions by one-half million tons over five years. Once the engineers took up the challenge, they found 2.2 million tons of savings in just two years.[7]

My company had a similar experience. We ran into an unending string of roadblocks as we tried to implement our stretch goals. We finally came up with the *Make Every Decision a Green Decision™* strategy because we couldn't find a better path. Either we couldn't get good enough information to guide our decision-making, or the options being proposed were too expensive. But when we looked back after just 15 months, we were stunned and gratified to discover how far we'd come, how little it had cost, and that we were already enjoying a net savings that would be sustained for years to come. Stories like this are pretty common because so much low-hanging fruit is waiting to be picked. It turns out that living with tradeoffs doesn't have to slow you down. On the other hand, giving up when things get messy, or waiting until you can deliver that one perfect punch before you even start swinging, will stall you out.

Going green generates its own momentum, largely because the towels we're carrying are sopping wet. Nobody wrings out a towel with just one twist. You always need to do it again.

There's just one more issue to address before getting down to brass tacks and specific recommendations. If you're going to set ambitious stretch goals, you'll need know what to measure, how to do it and what to make of those measurements.

Chapter Four

The Amazing Carbon Metric

With all that's been said already, it's no wonder there are so many different "shades of green." How can you compare reducing waste, for instance, with eliminating air pollution inside convention halls? You know going in that there must be several different ways to look for the best options, and you can bet some of the metrics are better than others. How can you make choices if you have to compare the proverbial apples to oranges all the time? Wouldn't it be better to have a single metric, just one number that helps the greenest opportunities stand out?

Say "Hello" to Carbon

The carbon footprint, which is often expressed in pounds, tons or kilograms of carbon dioxide (CO_2), or more broadly as all of the major greenhouse gases (CO_2e),[1] is becoming so commonplace in green business circles that many people would consider it the de facto environmental metric. You see carbon numbers popping up everywhere these days on corporate sustainability web pages. You can use any number of online carbon calculators to measure your household, your next vacation, your next new car and more. Some people are even pushing for carbon footprint labeling on consumer products.

If your company participates in ISO 14001, the Global Reporting Initiative, EPA Climate Leaders, The Climate Registry or any of several other environmental reporting programs, chances are pretty good that a colleague or consultant is estimating the company's greenhouse gas emissions too. They might well be measuring other things as well, such as resource consumption, landfill waste or toxic chemicals, but carbon offers something that these other metrics don't. Greenhouse gas emissions are a common denominator that every organization shares, and the relevance of carbon emissions to so many different business activities brings carbon closer than anything else to the Holy Grail of a single metric. It doesn't capture every environmental hazard by any means; no single metric ever could. But measuring carbon can tell you a lot of useful things about your events program, and where you might go looking for the Green Edge.

The reason this one metric has become so popular and pervasive is pretty simple: Carbon emissions are closely linked to energy, and it's easy to measure the energy used in a wide variety of activities. Gallons of gasoline, kilowatt-hours of electricity and therms of natural gas: Businesses measure energy all the time in order to pay bills, and experts have translated energy information into carbon pollution numbers. So whether or not climate change is high on your priority list, measuring greenhouse gas emissions has proven to be a very useful tool for a lot of applications. Think how confusing it would be if you had to compare kilowatt-hours (kWh) of electricity to British thermal units (BTU) of heat contained in a variety of fuels, or reduce all of them to joules, an underlying unit of energy or work. That's no problem for technically minded people, but companies are finding it more useful to report a unifying metric to their stakeholders. And for those of us who spend our days worrying about transportation and travel logistics, and exhibit production choices, the carbon metric simplifies the challenge considerably by reducing things to just one number.

Fortunately, carbon is also a pretty good tool for measuring some of the biggest environmental drivers in your events program. You can use carbon metrics to look at two broad and important categories in your day-to-day work. The first category includes transportation and travel: how you move people and properties to and from events. The second category involves the "embodied carbon" in the materials that are used to produce goods, which in your case means exhibits and associated properties. So let's take a look at how to use carbon metrics and see what they can tell us.

Fun with Numbers

The first and most important thing to know is that the carbon metric is not really intended to give you an absolute, literal picture of carbon pollution per se. Rather, the metrics are designed to help you *compare options*. You can assign carbon numbers to options A, B and C to figure which one will have the smallest environmental impact. For example, we can calculate that flying round trip from New York to an event in Las Vegas by way of a connection in Atlanta will emit about 12 percent more CO_2 than flying nonstop. It's the comparison, here, that's so useful. You don't even need to know what the total emissions numbers are to make an environmentally informed decision.

In the same way, you can calculate that driving solo from Los Angeles to that same Las Vegas event in a hybrid car will emit roughly the same amount of CO_2 as flying to the show in an airplane seat. It's very close to a 1:1 ratio. Of course, the hybrid still has three empty seats in it, so you could send up to four people in the car on the same carbon budget as the frequent flyer will spend.

At the same time, if you make the trip solo in an SUV you will emit roughly three-and-one-half times more carbon pollution than the hybrid driver or the airline passenger does; the SUV's carbon pollution ratio is about 3.5-to-1. The point in all this is that measuring carbon reveals choices in ways that you might not otherwise be able to see. And with nothing more than the information in this paragraph, you can now estimate that carpooling to Las Vegas with two coworkers in the SUV will emit just a little more CO_2 pollution per passenger than the person who goes by air. All you have to do is divide that 3.5-to-1 ratio by three passengers.

It's easy to get this information, and it's useful because driving one car is a lot less expensive than buying three airline tickets. And if you push the carpooling idea a whole lot further, the numbers also show that you could send nine people in three hybrids and still have a smaller impact in terms of total carbon emissions than the solo SUV driver will have. At a ratio of 3.5-to-1, three hybrids leave a smaller carbon footprint than one SUV. That's a big enough difference to raise questions about a company's overall event staffing and travel strategy. And, just to top it all off, it turns out that you could send eight hybrid cars carrying a total of 32 passengers from Los Angeles to the Las Vegas event on the same carbon budget as one lonely traveler spends flying nonstop from the Big Apple. That's impressive, and it is yet another demonstration that saving money and improving environmental performance go hand in hand no matter where you decide to draw the line between airplanes and carpools.

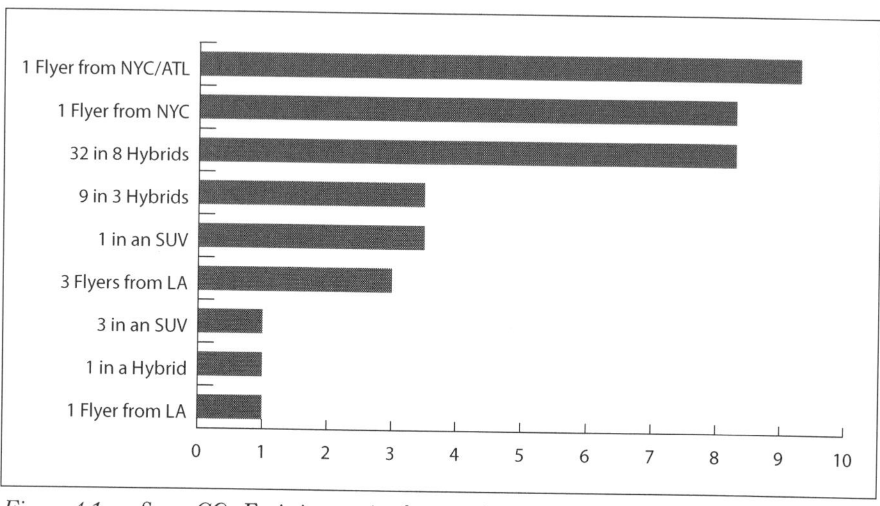

Figure 4.1 — Some CO_2 Emissions ratios for travel to an event in Las Vegas

Figure 4.1 shows all these ratios in a simple graph. This is a case where doing a few rough calculations begins to reveal ways in which you might start wringing carbon out of your event travel towel. So far, though, we've been concentrating primarily on travel strategies for a nearby show where carpooling is not only viable, it's actually quite commonplace. Many people prefer a few quiet hours on the road to the hustle and bustle hassles of getting through airports and renting cars. As you know the travel distances to most events exceed the practical limits for driving, and our simple graph of carbon emissions ratios has a lot to say about your flying options too.

As Figure 4.1 makes clear, you could fly three people from Los Angeles to the Las Vegas event on about the same carbon budget as sending one person alone in an SUV. That's the power of packing people into vehicles, and it applies to every mode of transportation: cars, trains, ships and airplanes. Later, we'll see that this same green principle applies to shipping properties as well, but let's get back to the people. How many staffers can you fly to the Las Vegas event from Los Angeles on the same carbon budget as the lone, weary New Yorker spends? If we're comparing

Los Angeles flights to a nonstop from New York, the answer is eight. But if the New Yorker has to make a connection through a hub in Atlanta along the way, the carbon emissions are equivalent to nine Angelinos flying off to Vegas. The ratios are 8-to-1 or 9-to-1, in this case, depending on the flight path. Let's unpack what this means.

The first message is that flying nonstop is always more eco-efficient than making connections. Every online travel calculator will prove this, and it's really no surprise because airplanes have to fly farther out of their way whenever connections are made. On top of this, airplanes burn much more fuel while climbing to altitude than when they're cruising along above the clouds, so it's always greener to climb once per journey than two or three times.

The second message is that long-distance flying is enormously costly in terms of people's time, your company's budget and environmental damage. In terms of sheer impact on your triple bottom line, it's hard to overstate the consequences of long-distance flights. In fact, they are probably the largest environmental factor in your entire events program, and it doesn't matter whether you build and ship exhibits to all those events or attend professional conferences that don't even have exhibit halls. Either way, the more time you spend measuring travel emissions, the more apparent this will become in your green thinking. Armed with this type of analysis, the Union of Concerned Scientists concluded: "After all, a single round-trip fight from Los Angeles to New York emits around a ton of carbon dioxide per passenger—equal to the amount an average American SUV driver would be responsible for emitting in a month of average driving."[2]

That's a big takeaway. "But," you say, "We really don't have a choice because our colleague from New York needs to be at the show." Fair enough, but remember the big idea: *When In Doubt, Zoom Out.*

It will be very difficult to find the Green Edge by looking at just one show in isolation because your options are so limited. Carbon comparisons become much more revealing when you examine the magnitude of your entire trade show or conference schedule at once. This is where you begin to see lots of people and properties traveling to and from many different destinations all the time. If you apply the simple carbon emission ratios in Figure 4.1 to a stretch goal that requires you to reduce emissions, you'll have to start asking some interesting and importation new questions.

For example: Does your colleague from New York really need to attend *every one of your events?* Could people who live and work closer to some of the event venues fill in just as effectively once in a while? After all, if the event is near the West Coast you can send a person by air from Los Angeles for just one-eighth the environmental cost and, presumably, a small fraction of the ticket price too.

This question isn't really any different from the one my company asked when we decided to reorganize visits to our fabrication partners. The carbon metric showed us that we could make enormous environmental gains by rethinking procedures in ways that we had never considered before. In fact, it was the carbon information that changed our priorities. When we combined what we were seeing in the CO_2 numbers with the lost productivity that came with spending so many hours driving the LA freeways, the idea of going about our work differently suddenly began to make sense. Obviously, your answers will depend on your circumstances, and whether local sales reps or colleagues from region offices or partner institutions can represent your interests on site. Whatever you decide, running the carbon numbers will give you and your team a new way to look at the costs and benefits of staffing events in different ways.

Don't be at all surprised to find that Green Edge advantages are multifaceted, just as they are for our company. Some executives and event professionals spend enormous amounts of time preparing for, traveling to and attending event after event after event. If that's their primary job, OK, but if they have other important things to accomplish besides sitting on airplanes, it's quite possible that they have simply slipped into patterns and sets of expectations that are neither green, nor especially satisfying or productive. Carbon metrics can be catalysts for productive change.

Notice that we've reached all of these conclusions without saying a word about the literal, absolute amounts of CO_2 that our weary travelers are pumping into the atmosphere. The quotation from the Union of Concerned Scientists gives the very first hint, in fact, that we're talking about significant numbers. It's the ratios that are most helpful when you want to compare things, and this is where carbon metrics really excel.

The only thing you have to be careful about is comparing apples to other apples and not to oranges, bananas or kiwis. Whenever you make comparisons, the first order of business is to be sure that you're measuring all of your options in the same way. Things tend to go haywire when you don't. Here's a case in point: A client of ours became irate one day when he thought his exhibit house was overcharging for storage. The supplier was billing 75 cents per square foot, and when the exhibitor learned that a competitor was offering storage at the bargain-basement rate of 14 cents per cubic foot, he hit the roof. Our client was blinded by the huge difference between the two numbers and he didn't really notice that the shops were actually measuring different things. So we sat down and figured it out. We took a typical storage space measuring 10' x 10'. That's 100 square feet, which we multiplied by his supplier's unit price and discovered that he was paying $75 to pile exhibits all the way up to the ceiling. The other shop was charging by the cubic foot, so the square we had just looked at was really a cube that contained 1,000 cubic feet. Multiplying by the unit price showed that if he switched shops, he'd pay $140 to stack his properties just 10 feet high. When we compared apples-to-apples, the exhibitor was greatly relieved to see that he was, in fact, getting a very good deal after all.

Another type of comparison error could easily start at home. If you weigh yourself on a bathroom scale every morning, you're comparing the same thing day after day after day: you always weigh yourself at more-or-less the same hour, you haven't eaten yet, and you aren't wearing any clothes. The only variable is whether you gained or lost a pound or two, so you can trust the results. But when you get weighed at your doctor's office, it could be any time of day, you might or might not have just eaten a big meal, and you might be wearing different clothes than you wore during your last visit. Does this make the doctor's measurements any less accurate than the ones you take at home? Certainly not: The scales they use are probably even better than the ones on your bathroom floor, but you can't possibly use your doctor's results to track your daily diet plan. Since your doctor only sees you once in a while, the measurements taken at the office aren't frequent enough or consistent enough to show whether you've gained or shed those pesky few pounds. You know this, of course, so if you and your doctor are tracking your diet together, you'll report what you see at home. The doctor knows all of this, too, and uses the office scale to determine whether your weight is basically where you'd like it to be, and whether it is following a larger trend over the years. Making comparisons is all about understanding the context in which the measurements are made, controlling the variables, picking the right tool for the job and learning what the results can tell you.

As it turns out, that's exactly what carbon measurements are all about too. Let's take a look at the two categories of interest to exhibitors and meetings managers—emissions from travel and transportation, and embodied emissions in materials—to see whether carbon metrics can reveal opportunities to reduce costs and go green.

Travel and Transportation: The Carbon You Burn

If we're going to make useful comparisons, we'll need reliable tools. For transportation, we can turn to the U.S. Environmental Protection Agency (EPA), which provides the emissions numbers that many travel-related carbon calculators rely on.[3] The EPA's carbon emission factors for transportation are widely used by state and local government agencies, nonprofit carbon offset providers and businesses because they provide the right tools for comparing the various ways in which we travel and ship goods. In other words, they are a standard reference for estimating travel emissions.

STEP ON THE BATHROOM SCALE FOR A CLOSE-UP VIEW

Let's start with something that's analogous to standing on your bathroom scale in the morning, which is where you make detailed, daily measurements, and then we'll zoom out to look at your larger travel and shipping concerns.

The EPA says that burning a gallon of gasoline emits 19.6 pounds of CO_2 and a gallon of diesel emits a little bit more: 22.4 pounds of CO_2.[4] These are so-called "tailpipe emissions" from the direct combustion of fuel in your car's engine. This means they don't include carbon dioxide from the activities that happened before you filled your tank. Those are called "Well-to-Pump" emissions, and they come from extracting the crude, shipping it to refineries around the world, turning it into fuel and distributing the fuel to your local gas station. The EPA numbers only cover the emissions that flow out of gasoline or diesel when you burn it in your car. So the numbers are accurate, even if they aren't complete.

The Union of Concerned Scientists took this on and determined that if you add tailpipe and Well-to-Pump estimates together, gasoline emits more like 25 pounds of CO_2 per gallon.[5] Should you use this number instead? No! You wouldn't want to change your metrics for just one type of fuel. You can't make useful comparisons unless you measure everything in the same way. Keep in mind that going green is all about making improvements by comparing greener options to what you're doing today; it isn't about cataloging every last absolute literal detail. Since the EPA provides a consistent set of metrics for cars, airplanes, ships and trains, it doesn't really matter whether they include Well-to-Pump emissions as long as the EPA uses the same procedures for every type of fuel. It's just like weighing yourself in the morning; as long as you do it the same way every day, you'll get the information you need to make progress on your diet. But it would be a mistake to weigh yourself with your clothes on every so often and think you were getting an honest comparison.

This, in fact, is the next all-important Big Idea: *Use Metrics to Compare Options.*

Let's return to that event in Las Vegas to see how the numbers work. To make this easy, suppose your car happens to get 19.6 mpg, which is somewhat below the national average for passenger cars. At 19.6 mpg it will emit one pound of CO_2 for every mile you drive. If you drive 500 miles, which is most of the way from Los Angeles to Las Vegas and back, it will emit 500 pounds of CO_2. If you add a second passenger on your 500-mile trip, each of you will travel the distance for half of the total emissions, or 250 pounds per person. With two in the car, your personal emissions become one-half pound per passenger mile. Carry four passengers and your number drops to one-quarter pound per passenger mile. That's how easy it is to calculate the benefits of carpooling.

But let's take it a step further: Suppose on your next 500-mile trip you have a choice of rental cars. The people at the rental counter offer you an eco-collection 2012 Toyota Prius hybrid, with an EPA estimated 50 mpg (that's combined highway and city), or a 2012 Toyota Sequoia SUV with an EPA estimated 14 mpg.[6] Let's run the carbon numbers. All you have to do is divide 500 miles by each vehicle's estimated mpg to figure how many gallons of gasoline it will burn and multiply those results by 19.6. In a perfect world, the Prius will use 10 gallons of gas and emit 196 pounds of CO_2 on your journey, whereas the Sequoia will burn 35.72 gallons and emit 700 pounds. This is very close to the somewhat simplified 3.5-to-1 ratio we looked at earlier.

What we're doing here is using a carbon emissions estimate *to compare different ways of doing exactly the same task*. It's an apples-to-apples comparison just like the daily progress reports you get each morning on your bathroom scale. You don't really know the total emissions for your 500-mile trip any more than you know your actual weight down to the last decimal point. Nor do you need to. A blip up or down on the scale will either give you good news or lead you to skip dessert for a few days. In the same way, this quick carbon estimate can help you decide which car to rent: the SUV or the one that emits 72 percent less CO_2. It's the comparison between one option and another, or between where you're standing and where you want to that informs your eco-decisions.

HEAD TO THE DOCTOR TO SEE THE BIG PICTURE

We just did a detailed calculation on a very small eco-challenge. Suppose you want to answer a slightly bigger question: Is there a more eco-efficient and cost-effective way to transport your staff when they are on show site? If your company has been renting cars at events, you might want to add up the costs and emissions and compare them to some alternatives, such as using public transportation or hiring vans. A small team might only rent one or two cars, or a larger team might rent more than 10 or 20. How would you make the estimate? If you try using the procedure we just looked at, you'll have to gather all the makes and models, find out which engine option each car has and run each of them through the EPA's *Green Vehicles Guide* website to learn its estimated fuel economy.[7] Then you'll need to find out how far each car was driven so you do to the calculations. Coping with so many details becomes an unworkable burden very quickly, so we need a more efficient way to make estimates that will show us what we want to know.

When the calculations become so complex that chasing the details isn't feasible, the only practical solution is to zoom out and look the bigger picture in the same way your doctor looks at your weight in a more general way. Zooming out involves rounding things off because you have fewer pieces of data to look at. But the rounding needs to be done in a way that doesn't hide the essential truth of the comparisons. Your doctor wants to know whether your weight is healthy, and you want to know whether your travel plans are sustainable.

The EPA's guidance to Climate Leaders solves this problem in an elegant way. While EPA provides carbon auditors with fairly detailed calculation procedures that don't suit our purposes, they also provide simplified carbon metrics for the rest of us to use. For drivers, the EPA uses national transportation statistics to estimate the average fuel economy of all of the passenger cars on the road today. This average is better than the Sequoia's mileage but it's nowhere near what the Prius delivers, so you can't use this number to decide which type of car to rent the next time you're standing at the rental counter. Instead, use it to decide how many cars to rent and how many passengers to pack into them. You can also use this number to compare driving with other modes of transportation.

For air travel, the EPA incorporates statistics that account for the different number of passengers on various types of aircraft and the average number of seats that go unsold. Because of the great efficiency differences involved, the EPA splits the emissions numbers into three categories: one for short-haul, another for medium-haul and a third for long-haul flights. Trains and ships get the same travel statistics treatment and the EPA offers average emissions per passenger mile for each mode. This means that the CO_2 numbers account for the fact that trains rarely run full, and if you choose to vote with your pocketbook, you can help increase the eco-efficiency of riding the rails in the same way that you can increase the efficiency of cars by carpooling. In other words, these larger scale statistics don't mean that you can't make greener personal choices to reduce emissions. Your doctor's overall view of your weight doesn't mean that you can't lose a pound or two if you want to; it just means that the few times you stand on the doctor's scale won't show your daily progress. In the same way, riding the rails more frequently will reduce transportation emissions, even though the estimates you make using these tools won't show those results.

If you want to run some numbers yourself, here are the EPA's simple CO_2 factors for passenger travel. Estimates are easy to make: Just look up the distance people will travel and multiply by the number of passengers, then multiply that result by the emission factors in the table on the next page. One word of caution, though: Use an online carbon calculator to look up flight distances because airplanes don't have to follow meandering roads and the driving directions you get from online maps will mislead you.[8]

Mode of Travel	lb CO_2 per passenger mile	kg CO_2 per passenger mile
Bus	0.24	0.107
Transit Rail (e.g., subways)	0.36	0.163
Commuter Rail	0.38	0.172
Intercity Rail (e.g., Amtrak)	0.41	0.185
Airline (>700 miles)	0.41	0.185
Airline (300 – 700 miles)	0.50	0.229
Airline (<300 miles)	0.61	0.277
Car	0.80	0.364

Table 4.2—EPA emissions factors for passenger travel[9]

By the way, some online emissions calculators offer an "RF" or "RFI" option for flight emissions, and you might have heard of this. These acronyms stand for "radiative forcing" and "radiative forcing index," and they refer to the additional warming effect caused by the water vapor, particulates and greenhouse gases that airliners emit at cruising altitudes. The best scientific estimate for the radiative forcing index is 2.7 times higher than the carbon emissions factors that you see in this table.[10] The science is still being researched, however, and the EPA does not include this factor in its calculations.

Leaving RFI aside, this table is really quite revealing. In Table 4.2, all you have to do is look at these emissions factors to understand the ratios. One person in an average car generates roughly twice the CO_2 as a passenger on a long-haul flight or an Amtrak train. If you flip back to Figure 4.1 you'll see that one passenger in a hybrid car was on par with one passenger on a medium-haul flight, and this gives you an indication of how much greener the most fuel efficient cars are than the national average.

If you compare riding the rails to flying, be sure to use the correct flight distance. Many people ride trains between New York and Washington, DC, for example, which should be compared to a medium-haul flight. In this case, trains beat airplanes even when they aren't full. But if you take the time to ride the train between Boston and Atlanta, compare your rail emission with a long-haul flight.

One other important factor might not be obvious in the table: the assumption that there is just one person in an average car. If you carpool with one other person, each of you will use half of the emissions factor in the table, and if the car has four occupants, each passenger would divide 0.80 by four. Remember, a more fuel-efficient car will beat these numbers every time, as will a fully loaded train.

We'll apply these emissions factors to an exhibitors travel strategy in the next chapter and see how easy it is to find big opportunities on the Green Edge.

SHIPPING: THE CARBON YOU SEND AWAY

Similar methods are used to estimate carbon emissions for shipping goods. The EPA provides a simplified number for one ton of cargo traveling one mile (a "ton-mile"). This means the EPA averages national transportation statistics for medium- and long-haul tractor-trailers. Trade show van lines tend to run newer, more fuel efficient fleets than you might find working construction sites, but this difference is lost for the sake of simplicity and for making useful comparisons with airfreight. As with automotive emissions, the EPA's simplified freight emissions factors won't help you make fine-grained choices between shipping companies, but they do make it easy to see the difference between sending properties by truck or by air.

If you'd like to calculate shipping options on your own, here are the simplified CO_2 factors for the various modes of transportation. The calculation is just as easy as it is for passenger travel: Just look up the travel distance and multiply it by the weight of your shipment, then multiply the result by the CO_2 factors in the table below.

Mode of Shipping	lb CO_2 per ton-mile	kg CO_2 per ton-mile
Train	0.056	0.0252
Ocean Freight	0.106	0.0480
Truck (tractor-trailer)	0.655	0.2970
Airfreight	3.366	1.527

Table 4.3—EPA emissions factors for shipping goods[11]

The striking thing in this table is the enormous difference between trucking and airfreight. We'll come back to this difference when we look for greener shipping options in the following chapters.

We've been exploring carbon metrics at different scales in order to make appropriate comparisons. In the carpooling calculation we zoomed in on a small eco-challenge to get a close-up view. The rounded off emissions factors in these tables obscure those fine-grained details in order to bring clarity to the bigger picture, which involves the different modes of transportation. You can't use close-up calculations to address complex scenarios, nor can you use the rounded-off emissions factors to split hairs. Interpreting carbon metrics is all about matching the right tool to the right job. As you zoom farther and farther out and take in a larger view, your estimates will become increasingly imprecise. That's just the nature of estimating: we see it with budgets and project timelines, and it's no different with carbon metrics.

Which brings us to the sixth Big Idea: *The Rougher the Estimate, the Greener the Difference Needs to Be.*

Construction Materials: The Carbon You Embody

If you want to measure the carbon emissions associated with your exhibit booth and other properties, this Big Idea about rough estimates should be your guiding principle. Calculating carbon emissions for transportation is comparatively easy because trains, plains and automobiles literally burn the fuels that release CO_2 as they move around. EPA limits the CO_2 factors that we use in our calculations to this direct combustion of fuels, which makes the calculations, results and reporting process fairly straightforward. My company sees these terms, in fact, in the reports we receive annually from The Climate Registry, in which "Greenhouse Gas Emissions from Direct Combustion of Fuels" is one of the categories.

That's not the case with the emissions that are said to be "embodied" in construction materials and products. One reason for this is that there are complicated intermediate steps in the use of energy to extract raw materials and convert them into useful products. When a mill turns ore into metal or a factory turns logs into plywood, for example, it uses electricity, among other forms of energy. So the carbon emissions from generating that electricity need to be included in the equations that describe the carbon pollution that becomes embodied in the end products. Electricity is generated by burning coal, which emits a great deal of carbon, or oil or natural gas, or by any of several other processes including nuclear fission, hydropower, wind, geothermal and solar. Each source has a different carbon emissions profile, and some generating stations are more efficient than others as well. On top of that, mills and factories often use multiple sources of energy, including direct combustion of fuels and electric power, and some plants even recycle and use waste heat. Other plants might not be so energy efficient. This means that the carbon emissions from industrial processes can vary considerably from one facility to another around the world. You can see the challenge, but we're not finished yet.

Some of the materials used to build exhibit booths in the United States are manufactured domestically. Aluminum is an example of a material in which most U.S. production is consumed domestically. Other materials are more globalized, and there's nothing to say that the particular piece of aluminum extrusion, acrylic, plywood or steel didn't come from a far-away source. This doesn't really mean that the transportation of materials from the factories to your exhibit shop is a major factor. In most cases transportation is a lesser issue. Rather, it means something that might not be obvious at all: There is wide variation in how carefully factories and mills track and report their energy use and carbon emissions. The range extends from no record keeping at all in some corners of the world to fairly strict reporting requirements within the European Union. But even in Europe, most reporting is for an overall facility and not to the level of detail that reveals the emissions for specific products.[12] When record keeping is spotty, experts pick the best data they can find and extrapolate in order to estimate the averages. This last point is not so different from EPA's reliance on national transportation statistics to come up with average passenger and freight emissions factors, except that there are many fewer data points for materials researchers to work with.

How would you come up with a set of carbon emissions factors for construction materials in the face of so many complicated challenges? As we learned with the bathroom scale analogy, you have to use the right tool for each job. You can't extrapolate a person's day-to-day weight from the occasional visits to the doctor. In the world of embodied materials, this translates into setting boundaries around the things that you can measure reasonably well.

What we're really talking about here is conducting a Life-Cycle Assessment (LCA) of the carbon emissions that occur in manufacturing materials. All of the emissions caused by extracting the raw materials and turning them into useful products, such as sheets of plywood and rolls of carpet, are said to be embodied in those materials themselves. When you, the exhibitor, buy an exhibit, you essentially take ownership of and responsibility for those embodied carbon missions because your purchasing decision is responsible for those emissions having occurred. It's a clever way to account for the carbon pollution that goes into products, and the Life-Cycle Assessment process is quite rigorous. Here is a brief description based on the international standard for Life-Cycle Assessments, ISO 14040:

> The ISO standard assumes that LCA is used for comparing two similar ways to complete the same product. A boundary is defined round a system which is broad enough to encompass all differences between the alternative products. Every process within this boundary is examined and numerical values are calculated for drivers of any environmental concern within the boundary, for the two approaches. The LCA study then calculates the difference between the two approaches, and anticipates how this will lead to environmental harm. This approach is clearly defined and rigorous.[13]

The whole trick in doing Life-Cycle Assessments that give dependable, comparable results is in getting the boundaries right. And as we saw with the EPA's transportation emissions, you have to set the boundaries and do the analysis consistently for all of the materials you want to compare: Otherwise, your comparisons won't mean anything. One of the best sources of LCA data on construction materials comes from the Sustainable Energy Research Team at the University of Bath in the United Kingdom. Their careful analysis of global LCA data led to one of the most rigorous and careful boundary setting efforts, and the University of Bath's *Inventory of Carbon and Energy (ICE)* is an international reference.[14] Through their good efforts, it quickly becomes clear that the number of quality data points varies from one material to the next and, second, that a great deal of the best data comes from Europe, where energy and carbon reporting are required.

These restrictions led the team at the University of Bath to limit embodied carbon data on construction materials to what is called a "Cradle-to-Gate" assessment.

You've probably heard of Cradle-to-Grave and Cradle-to-Cradle approaches to sustainability. The basic idea is that we should consider the full lifespan of a product when we evaluate its environmental impacts, including drilling, mining, logging and conversion to materials; product assembly; our use of the finished products; and, ultimately, disposal methods. An ideal LCA would cover everything from end to end. But we can't do that for construction materials if we want to make useful comparisons. The best data supports placing the boundary of the Life-Cycle Assessment on the loading dock of the mill or factory that turns raw materials into construction materials.

A lot of folks are concerned that Cradle-to-Gate ignores the carbon that is emitted when construction materials are shipped from those loading docks to distributors and ultimately to exhibit shops. But the researchers suggest that we should not worry so much about this omission when we compare materials, and there are two specific reasons for saying so. The first is that, as always, our goal is to compare products in order to make greener choices. If we don't have good shipping emissions data for some of the products, then we need to set the boundary where reasonable comparisons can be made. Moreover, the distances that materials travel can mislead you:

> A common mistake made by the public is to assume that local agricultural products have less of a carbon footprint than those shipped from overseas manufacturing and farming locations. This is nicely illustrated by analyzing the carbon footprint of a bottle of wine sold in New York City. A typical bottle produced in the Loire Valley in France generates 45 percent less carbon dioxide than the one produced in Napa Valley, California. The reason is that the French bottle is shipped mostly over the ocean while the California wine is trucked—two modes of transportation that differ significantly in carbon efficiency.[15]

Not only do distance and modes of transportation vary, it's also true that so-called "Gate-to-Site" transportation emissions tend to be a very small part of the overall emissions picture for most of the materials exhibit houses use. In the case of wine, the amount of energy going into making the product is relatively small compared to transporting the product, but the situation is reversed for most of the materials used in exhibitry. The folks at the University of Bath ran the numbers and concluded: "In many cases, and certainly for materials with high embodied energy and high density, the difference between Cradle-to-Gate and Cradle-to-Site could be considered negligible."[16]

Nearly all of the materials in your exhibits tend to fit this description. And given the wide variations in where materials might come from, and the modes of transportation that might be used, it makes a lot more sense to run embodied carbon comparisons on the materials themselves at the manufacturer's gate.

Attempting to determine the sources for each material you are considering for your next build would be a lot like trying to look up the fuel efficiency of every rental car hired at an event. Plywood is produced in Canada, the Pacific Northwest, the Northeast, the South, China, Brazil, Europe and elsewhere, and because it is a commodity product, your shop's distributor might buy it from different sources on different days. Metals and plastics fall into the same boat, and even if you know that one source is domestic while another is international, you probably don't know whether the materials traveled by truck or by train. In the end, you can make much more efficient comparisons using Cradle-to-Gate LCAs.

With all of these caveats, can we really make useful embodied carbon estimates for exhibits? Yes, indeed, and if your exhibit partner can give you a detailed bill of materials for your next project, it's quite easy to run the numbers. All you have to do is multiply the total weight of each material in the proposed design by the emissions factors in the University of Bath ICE. Voilá! You'll have a result that you can compare to alternative combinations of materials. We'll do this in the next chapter, but we need to consider one additional source of carbon in your events program first.

Hotels: The Carbon You Sleep With

Hotels use a lot of energy, and higher-end and business-class hotels tend to use more energy than do other classes of hotels. The EPA provides carbon emissions estimates on the basis of a hotel room night. Once again, these are average emissions factors for hotels across the country, in different climate conditions and in buildings of all ages. The average for all classes of hotels is 65.1 pounds of CO_2 per room night and the average for higher-end and business-class hotels is 73.6 pounds of CO_2 per room night.[17]

These two numbers make calculating hotel emissions for an event very easy. To estimate CO_2 emissions for your team's hotel rooms, simply multiply the number of rooms you'll need by the number of nights you'll use them, and then multiply the result by the appropriate emissions factor. If you have 10 people, for example, staying five nights in a business class hotel, the estimated carbon footprint is 10 x 5 x 73.6 = 3,680 pounds of CO_2.

You know the drill by now: These are very rough averages that can only be used to make decisions about the total number of rooms and nights you want to book. You can't possibly identify or select a green hotel using this tool. In fact, the EPA advises that emissions vary quite a bit according to the local climate and the demand for heating and air conditioning, and whether a particular hotel has installed high-efficiency, state-of-the-art equipment or is relying on older equipment that could be upgraded. Even so, adding hotel room emissions to your planning matrix is a snap.

Greenwash: The Misuse and Abuse of Carbon Metrics

OK, so we've made carbon measurements look easy, which it is, and it's the simplicity of the carbon metric that makes it so useful for comparing options. But all of that apparent simplicity also makes carbon metrics very easy to abuse. And, oh, how people abuse them! Measuring and reporting carbon emissions is one of those areas where both accidental and intentional misrepresentations are widespread, so it would be wise to inoculate ourselves against the two most flagrant forms of carbon greenwash.

MISUSE OF INPUT-OUTPUT ANALYSIS

Here is one type of abuse: In the introduction I said that the meetings and corporate events industry in the United States "has a significant environmental footprint." That's true enough but the word "significant" is open to interpretation. Suppose I had tried to quantify its size instead. How could I have done it?

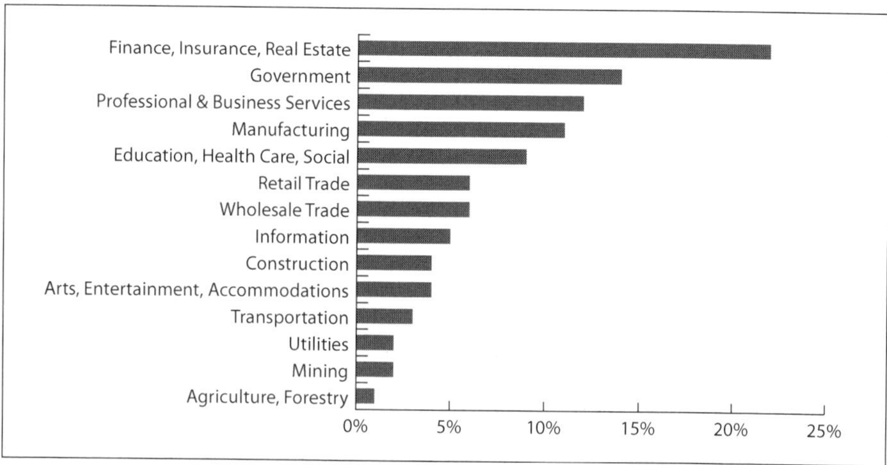

Figure 4.4 — U.S. GDP in 2009 broken down by industry[18]

Figure 4.4 shows a breakdown of U.S. gross domestic product by industry. The first thing you'll notice is that our industry doesn't appear on the list. Meetings and event planners make use of many sectors of the economy including manufacturing, transportation, entertainment and more, but the way economists keep track of things is more like your doctor's approach to watching your weight than it is to your own.

Suppose I decided to estimate the industry's carbon footprint for myself by doing a little simple arithmetic. I can look up the nation's total greenhouse gas emissions, which in 2011 were 7,387,945,290 tons of CO_2e.[19] The nation's GDP was $16.245 trillion[20] around that time, so some quick division seems to show that the American economy had a carbon intensity of about 0.9 pounds of CO_2e per dollar. Now, which estimate for the meeting and event industry's size should I use, $253 billion in direct spending or $907 billion in direct, plus indirect contributions to the gross domestic product? The results will obviously be quite different; they are either about 240 million tons or 410 million tons of CO_2e. Is one more accurate than the other?

Well, imagine going to your doctor on a nice summer day. You've been exercising and eating well, you've lost a few pounds and you're feeling full of vigor. Since it's a warm day, you aren't wearing heavy clothes, and you can't wait to hop up on the scale and impress everyone. But when you walk into the doctor's office you don't see any scale. So you ask where it went and the nurse says, "Oh, we got rid of our scale. We just divided the average weight of all Americans by their average height and that told us how much Americans weigh per inch. We know your height from your medical history—see, it's right here—so now we just multiply. It's so much easier than having to weigh patients all the time."

This is ridiculous on the face of it, right? Would you trust a doctor who can't recognize that some people are heavy and some people are thin? The same is true of industries. Not only can't you see the last few pounds you shed in the nurse's overly simplistic calculation, you can't even see someone you recognize. It's the same way with our little exercise in carbon intensity per dollar. If every supplier, every exhibitor and every meeting organizer in our industry takes the bull by the horns and slashes their carbon footprints in half, will their inspiring achievements show up in my calculation? No, because the metrics I used don't allow us to make this or any other type of useful comparison. It's the wrong tool for the job, so you shouldn't trust the results it gives. Whenever someone makes a definitive statement about the size of a carbon footprint, always ask yourself, *compared to what?*

Think back to the popular industry myth that opened this book. It's the one that says, ". . . trade shows are the second biggest source of commercial waste in the United States." It's a tenacious idea with tremendous staying power despite widely published rebuttals. I doubt this myth would have been so memorable if it had taken a slightly less definitive form, as in, "trade shows are big sources of commercial waste." Numbers are sticky. The carbon numbers I came up with for this industry, inaccurate though they clearly are, might have stuck with you too. Together, we might have launched a new urban myth. But it truly would have been a myth. This dollars-to-carbon type of estimate is useful for tracking a national economy and large sectors of an economy, such as the energy sector, industrial sector, agricultural sector and transportation sector. Dollars-to-carbon estimates work on a grand scale because people keep records of where energy is bought and sold, plus other important details. But you can't use this approach to measure the footprint of one industry, much less a single product, because nobody keeps track of all the fine details that would have to be accounted for.

Two University of Cambridge engineers explain the frequent misuse of the so-called "Input-Output" (IO) analysis this way:

> Unfortunately, assigning emissions to money flows can be quite misleading, and while the IO approach is logically consistent, it requires a huge data set, which is generally unavailable in sufficient detail, or for recent years. The analysis is performed for sectors, so cannot create results for individual products.[21]

And yet people make this mistake all the time, as I just demonstrated. Here's a particularly famous case of misusing the IO model: Do you recall hearing that a Hummer H2 causes less environmental damage than a Toyota Prius? A claim like this seems absurd on the surface, but it made the rounds based on a 2007 report by an automotive industry market research firm.[22] In their report, the researchers converted the dollars spent developing the two vehicles into energy and from there the numbers could be roughly converted into carbon emissions. Since the Prius incorporated a lot of new technology, its development costs were high, whereas the Hummer shared its tried and true platform with millions of other General Motors SUVs and trucks. So the disparity in development costs led to the conclusion that a Prius embodied more energy and, therefore, more carbon. Going a step further, this embodied carbon was amortized over the number of vehicles sold in order to get carbon-per-vehicle figures. Being relatively new, this meant the high development costs of the Prius were shared by a small number of cars, whereas the relatively low costs for the H2 was spread over a very large pool of vehicles. You can see where this is leading, but the researchers made one more interesting move: They decided that most of a vehicle's emissions occur during construction and not when customers are driving down the road. In fact, the opposite is the case.[23] And the numbers aren't even close. A study commissioned by the California Air Resources Board shows that emissions are overwhelmingly concentrated during the driving phase of a car's life no matter whether the car is powered by gasoline, electricity or a hybrid of both. Ninety-six percent of a gasoline-powered car's emissions occur on the road; it's 91 percent for a hybrid and 69 percent for a battery-powered electric car.[24]

Nevertheless, I still hear people proclaiming that hybrids are secret environmental hazards because results of this flawed study stuck. Was the original reporting a case of naïve analysis or intentional greenwash?

MISUSE OF LIFE-CYCLE ASSESSMENTS

This next, and even more common type of greenwashing is based on ignoring one of our Big Ideas: *Use Metrics to Compare Options.* To emphasize the point, the mantra could be rewritten to say *Use Metrics to Compare. Period.*

We've already seen that zooming out far enough to capture the embodied carbon in materials involves a lot of rounding off and estimating. We know that a lot of this estimating has to be done based on relatively few data points. It's the same way with your doctor's record of your weight: It's based on seeing you only a few times each year with your clothes on. There is no way for your doctor to make a definitive statement about your absolute, literal weight, and the same goes for Life-Cycle Assessments. But, as our two Cambridge engineers observe, it's easy to forget that LCAs are only valid for making comparisons:

> Unfortunately, almost all current users of the LCA method fail to apply it correctly as a comparison, and instead claim that it predicts the absolute impacts associated with a particular product. It doesn't, and as a result, almost all recently published LCA studies are misleading. They are so dependent on the boundaries used that they can be manipulated to create any answer. We have yet to find a single LCA study in which the company who paid for the study is responsible for the largest environmental impact.[25]

There it is. Whether it's by design or not, people who commission LCAs can easily move the boundaries around to the point that your product's environmental footprint is mostly somebody else's problem. For example, you could set the boundary to exclude the way electricity is generated, so the responsibility for those emissions fall on the energy sector instead of your product. You could exclude distribution of your product if that makes it look too carbon-intensive, and we haven't even discussed a host of complicating factors involving forests, minerals and resource extraction. And you could tell your doctor that you're wearing particularly heavy shoes today and that's the reason your weight appears to be going up as well.

This is why the experts at Cambridge advise people to use caution when they hear claims about a product's environmental footprint. Computers, video screens, furniture, carpet or exhibits: It just isn't appropriate to give a definitive carbon footprint number to any of these things. The only reasonable response to such claims is, compared to what?

As a counterpoint, you might have heard about carbon-neutral products. In these cases, manufacturers are supposed to conduct careful LCAs and implement production changes to reduce emissions from their supply chains and manufacturing processes. If carbon emissions cannot be eliminated entirely, a company might purchase carbon offset credits, which are also called "Renewable Energy Credits" (RECs) to make up for the difference. The carbon offsets are used to develop forests and other projects that will remove as much CO_2 from the atmosphere as the remaining manufacturing processes emit. So a carbon-neutral product does not have to be a zero-carbon product, but the net carbon transaction is supposed to balance out. Again, the evaluation involves setting boundaries and making comparisons.

In practical terms, even when you are dealing with honest brokers a trustworthy LCA is a partial picture from the environment's point of view. As amazing and useful as carbon metrics are—and they truly are—they don't account for every possible environmental consequence. This is why the European Life-Cycle Assessment website cautions:

> However, it has to be kept in mind that the use of LCA is merely a decision supporting tool, rather than a decision making tool, since it has a specific focus. It particularly tends to exclude economic and social impacts, as well as the consideration of more local environmental issues. It is therefore necessary to use it in conjunction with other tools to assist in identifying areas of potential improvement.[26]

This is good advice, and it helps explain why exhibitors often get hung up on dilemmas that carbon metrics can't answer. For example: Is it greener to present graphics on a video screen or print them on paper over and over again? As you can see by now, the LCA boundaries won't let us answer this question definitively. Is it greener to use a renewable resource, such as lumber, or a mineral resource that can be recycled, such as aluminum? The answer to this question reaches beyond carbon metrics as well because it extends into the worlds of ecosystem health and biodiversity, air and water pollution and other environmental concerns. Is bamboo, which grows much faster than hardwood, a greener choice than lumber? These are all legitimate questions, yet they reach beyond the limits of carbon measurement.

And it is the carbon metric's limitations that make it so useful for identifying certain types of eco-efficiency gains. In fact, no other environmental metric even comes close. So the bottom line on metrics is this: Use carbon emissions to compare alternative approaches to transportation, travel and construction materials.

In the next chapter you will see how revealing this exercise can be, and how it can help your program find the Green Edge. But we won't stop there because the advice from the European Commission is exactly right. Following our carbon case study we will look at some simple, straightforward guidance about reducing your event program's impacts on a range of other environmental and social issues.

Chapter Five

A Carbon Case Study

The powerful value proposition for carbon metrics is that they can reveal large opportunities that you might not otherwise see and lead your company to winning combinations of financial savings and eco-rewards. Let's review the Big Ideas and apply them to a real-world trade show program using what we've learned about carbon metrics to see whether we can unearth some big, green opportunities.

Just Wring Out the Waste.

With so much waste built into standard operating procedures, look for ways to reduce costs and make big environmental gains just by wringing it out.

When In Doubt, Zoom Out.

When you get stuck on the horns of a green dilemma, zoom out to see the bigger picture. Combinations of green choices often yield bigger gains.

Be Bold. Do the Impossible.

The most successful business-sustainability programs are driven by seemingly impossible goals that inspire innovation. It pays to be bold, not shy.

Go Public. Let Teamwork Pull You Forward.

You don't have to do it all by yourself. In a service-oriented industry like this, teamwork can move the needle faster than you might imagine.

Use Metrics to Compare Options.

Carbon metrics excel at helping you compare options and discover green opportunities that you might not be able to see otherwise.

The Rougher the Estimate, the Greener the Difference Should Be.

Estimates help you simplify, so you won't get lost in the weeds. When you simplify, focus your attention on seeking bigger gains.

A Carbon Case Study

A theme runs through the Big Ideas, which is to get you thinking beyond the fine points in order to explore the bigger picture. The next step is to examine real-world scenarios, and see whether we can find ways to improve sustainability and cut costs on a large scale. The case study in question is based on an actual trade show program. Even though some adjustments were necessary to fill in gaps where proprietary corporate information is not public knowledge, the program has not been idealized to make finding green choices easier. Realism is the crucial test because finding opportunities in the work you're actually doing is what going green is all about.

THE CASE STUDY

- Annual Show Schedule: three significant shows, one each in Los Angeles, Chicago and Washington-Baltimore.
- Exhibit: custom 300 square foot island exhibit (10' x 30') built using standard wood construction with a large storage room; a reception counter; large, graphic murals; small, product-specific graphics; several large, acrylic panels in aluminum frames with metal product display brackets; a small, signage header; seating and carpet.
- Audiovisual: none.
- Transportation: the exhibit ships in 10 crates, plus one carpetbag on an annual circuit with in-route storage between shows. The booth returns to the exhibit house annually for off-season storage and refurbishment.
- Updates: small, product-specific graphics are updated show-by-show; otherwise, the booth remains unchanged.
- Lifecycle: the exhibit is in service for at least 10 years without significant repairs or upgrades, yielding at least 30 events.

- Staffing: two exhibit managers travel from the Southeast and six sales representatives and executives travel from various locations: two from the Southeast, two from New England, one from the Midwest and one from the West.

The goal of this case study is to look across the major categories of exhibit-management responsibility, so let's begin with a snapshot of the exhibitor's current program. As you'll see a bit later, we are putting the EPA's travel, hotel and transportation emissions factors to work alongside the University of Bath's embodied carbon factors for construction materials.

Let's revisit the basics before we dive in, the first of which is that our goal is to find opportunities to go green *within each of these categories.* We are not trying to create a catalog of the program's total emissions per se, since our tools were not designed for that purpose. The value of totaling all of our discoveries at the end of this exercise will be in comparing the Green Edge potential with what the exhibitor is doing today. We will discover that potential by looking only inside the analysis of each category, so this will be our focus.

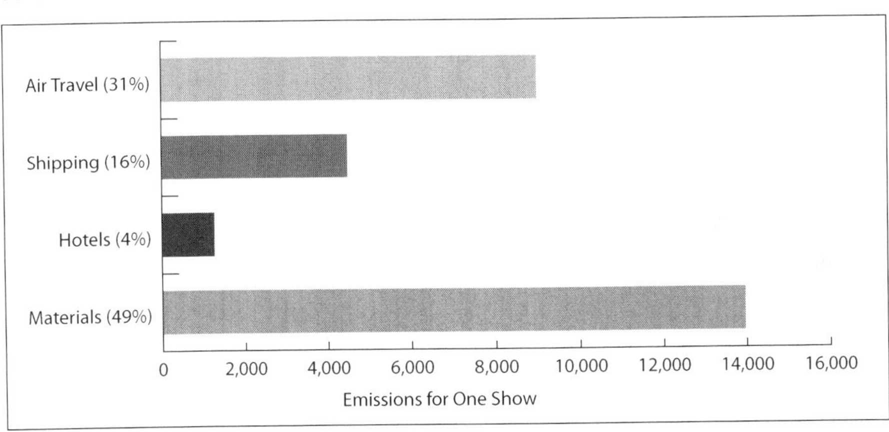

Figure 5.1 — Emissions for one show in pounds of CO_2 (materials in CO_2e)

The second point is that these metrics are used to make plans rather than account for the past. *This is a forward-looking process.* As you know all too well, executives are liable to pop in to some shows without warning and skip others, and you will contend with any number of other unexpected, real world surprises as you implement your green plans. So the actual performance of your program on the show floor—both its past performance and its future performance—might not match these planning scenarios to the last decimal place. But this is familiar territory to every manager because the same can be said for budgets, project timelines, and all of the other planning tools exhibitors and industry suppliers use to do their work.

Now that we're oriented to the task at hand, we can begin. Figure 5.1 summarizes the results for our carbon analysis for an average show in the exhibitor's annual schedule. The graph presents the categories side-by-side, so we won't accidentally trick ourselves into thinking that we are cataloging the total carbon footprint.

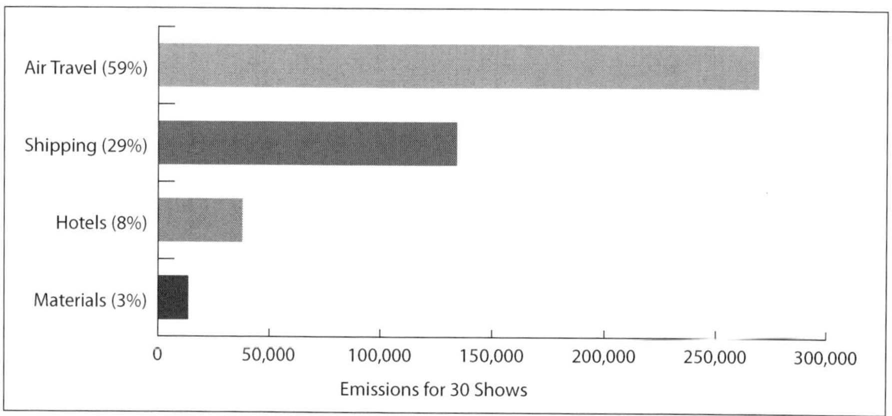

Figure 5.2 — Emissions for various activities over 30 events in pounds of CO_2 (materials in CO_2e)

You can see how important the embodied carbon from construction looks compared to emissions from travel, shipping and hotels in this graph, and this is a bit of a red herring. I've allocated all of the embodied carbon in the construction materials to this particular show, so there will be zero materials emissions henceforth at all future events. The preferred practice is to amortize the embodied carbon for materials across all of the events in the exhibit's lifetime, which includes at least 30 shows in this case study. Figure 5.2 presents the conventional approach to amortizing construction emissions. As you can see, choosing greener materials looks downright trivial in this presentation, even though the embodied carbon for the booth includes seven tons of CO_2e.[1]

But the truth is, for all of the attention green materials receive, embodied carbon emissions only occur once in an exhibit's lifetime. The other carbon-emitting activities recur at each and every show. The message here is clear: Going green isn't all about the booth. Don't overlook construction, of course, but anything you can do to reduce recurring environmental and financial costs from shipping and travel will pay dividends show after show after show, year after year after year. A new green booth might earn your company some great headlines, but don't miss the enormous opportunities that are hiding behind the scenes.

Comparing Construction Options

Let's turn our attention to options within each category, starting with construction. In this case study we will compare two different ways of building the same design. The first option is the "hard-wall" construction that the exhibitor is currently using, and it is the industry's most common approach. The second option is to build the same design using aluminum struts and stretched fabric to replace the hard plywood walls, while keeping some of the other features, such as the plywood reception counter.

We can use the University of Bath *Inventory of Energy & Carbon (ICE)* data to create a Cradle-to-Gate comparison between the two options. One of the advantages this gives us is simplicity since we won't have to try and chase down the actual factories and mills where each of the materials is created and the methods that are used to ship them to the exhibit house. Cradle-to-Gate analysis eliminates this unworkable complexity, just as EPA's travel emissions factors save us from having to look up the technical details on each and every rental car that the staff uses at the events. Since most of the materials under consideration have high levels of embodied carbon, this simplification will not make a significant difference in our results. Similarly, our comparison will not include carbon emissions that are generated by the exhibit house itself when the cabinetmakers and artisans build the booth. Here, again, we don't need to worry because the shop will work on the project in either case. So these emissions, or the lack of them, will not influence our results in favor of one choice over the other. In the end, our analysis of embodied carbon will be a fair, apples-to-apples comparison between the materials themselves, and the Cradle-to-Gate boundaries that the experts at the University of Bath have given us will simply increase the clarity of our choices.

To begin, the builder provides detailed bills of materials for both options in the case study, including the aluminum and fabric version that has never been built. A quick conversion is necessary in order to run the numbers, though, because the University of Bath ICE gives embodied carbon factors on the basis of each material's weight, whereas the shop buys materials on the basis of their dimensions. So, this step involves estimating the weight of each material that will be used to build the booth. The builder can gather some of this information from materials catalogs and the rest by weighing actual pieces. Once you've been through this process together you can use these weight factors for any and all future carbon comparisons you might want to do. Without very much effort you'll have what you need: two inventories—one for each option—that provide the total weights of each material under consideration, from plywood to aluminum to carpet and so forth.

We don't live in a perfect world, of course. In fact, the exhibit industry is something of a world unto itself. Our methods and materials draw heavily on standard resources in the construction industry, but we also combine them with a wide range of other specialty items that come from other domains. So it happens that our case study project uses a few materials that are not typically used to build buildings and these materials do not appear in the University of Bath database. We don't have emission factors for them. The question is whether these gaps will influence the comparisons we are making, and the answer, once again, is no. One of the materials is the foam pad under the carpet. Since this will be part of both options, its absence will not make any difference in our comparison. The other missing materials are printing paper for graphic murals and some of the finishes. The total weight for these items is extremely small, so we'll take note of them for now and see whether they are likely to interfere with our assessments after we run the numbers.

Figure 5.3 shows a breakdown of the materials used to build the exhibitor's hard-wall booth. As you can see, wood is the largest contributor to embodied carbon. The category includes the plywood and stick lumber used to build the walls, reception counter and shipping crates. The second largest contributor is plastic, which includes frosted acrylic panels and the PVC sheets that carry the graphics. Flooring is a commercial carpet; aluminum refers to support rails for the acrylic panels and brackets for the header and display shelves. Steel is a miscellaneous estimate that covers cabinet hardware, nuts and bolts and the like. A 15 percent contingency is added to account for the items that are not in the Bath database and other things that might have been overlooked. The sum of these embodied emissions is about 14,000 pounds of CO_2e. Keep in mind that this number is intended for comparison purposes.

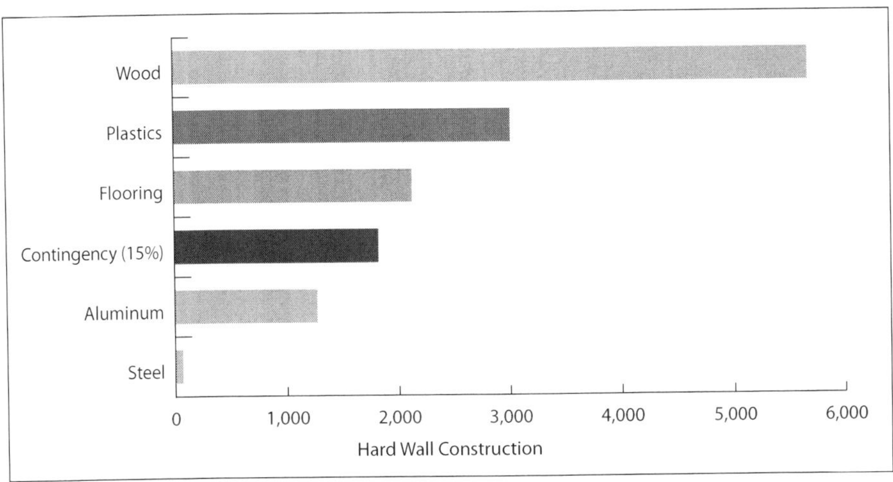

Figure 5.3 — Embodied carbon for the hard-wall option in pounds of CO_2e

Suppose the exhibit is built using the aluminum frame and stretched fabric option instead of hard walls. So-called "tension fabric" is a popular alternative. It is built on the same principles as a freestanding tent: The framework and fabric collapse into a much smaller package for shipping and storage. In this scenario, an aluminum and fabric version of the exhibit travels in just four crates instead of 10.

To render our hard-wall design in textiles, we are not really utilizing tension fabric to the fullest. Instead, fabric replaces plywood and PVC to create the storage room, signage header and large murals. Fabric also replaces the acrylic display panels, although the aluminum frames and wooden display shelves are retained, as are the plywood reception counter, carpet and seating. Figure 5.4 presents the differences between the hard-wall and tension-fabric approaches to building this design.

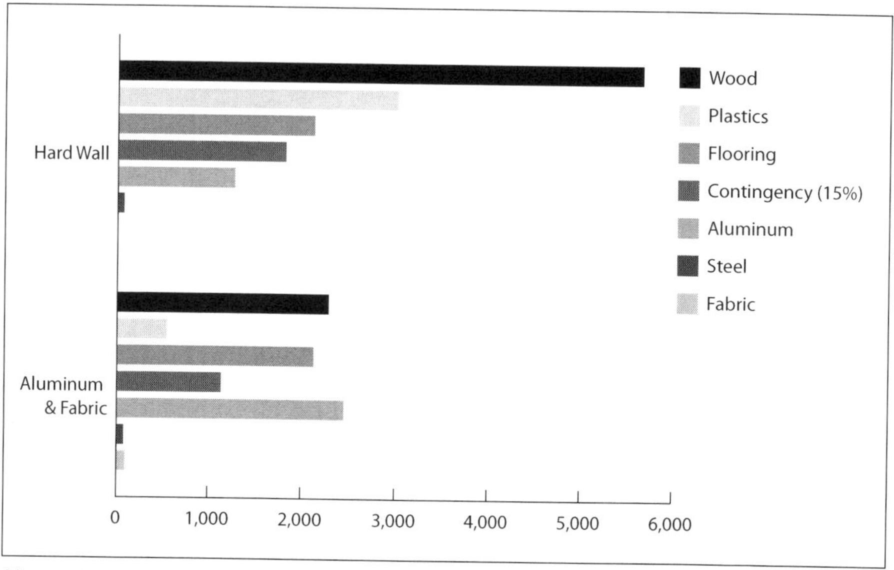

Figure 5.4 — Embodied emissions for alternative construction materials in pounds of CO_2e

You can see that the emissions from wood and plastic are reduced considerably, while the emissions from aluminum roughly double. Embodied carbon in the polyester fabric contributes very, very little: about one percent. Studying the University of Bath data on other types of paper, one may conclude that the missing murals in the hard-wall option would be negligible as well.

The difference between the two approaches is substantial: 14,000 pounds of CO_2e for hard walls versus 8,700 pounds for aluminum and textiles. Switching from hard wall to tension fabric, in this particular scenario, yields a 38 percent reduction in embodied carbon. On the financial side, by eliminating six crates, the low-carbon winner also saves somewhere in the neighborhood of $9,000 right out of the gate, even before the shop estimates the cost difference for the build. And this particular cost reduction will lead to further savings on shipping and drayage at every future trade show.

You can certainly run additional scenarios and you would probably want to. For one thing, because tension fabric and hard panel exhibits are very different animals, designers would not simply reproduce a hard-wall design in a different material. Hard walls look and feel substantial, and their forms favor straight lines and simple curves. Tension fabric, on the other hand, excels at freeform expression, and the materials inherently generate compound curves. So designers will naturally come up with a different design for the textile booth, and that is the design you want to compare with the hard-wall version. As the exhibitor, you also want to ensure that the fabric design meets your performance specifications for secure storage, brand image, durability and other factors while helping to achieve your sustainability goals. For example, it would be savvy to estimate the replacement cost for fabric skins and murals as part of the overall comparison because they are unlikely to outlast hard walls and rigid graphics. After all, this is not a sales pitch for one type of exhibit versus another. The *Make Every Decision a Green Decision™* mantra is about achieving your performance objectives with tactics that reduce your environmental impact, so you'll want to consider all of the relevant factors.

Bottom line: There is enough potential here for emissions reductions to warrant a careful look next time you consider building new properties.

Comparing Shipping Strategies

The exhibitor is already doing a good job of minimizing transportation emissions by routing the booth from show to show without sending it back to the Los Angeles-based exhibit house in between events. Figure 5.5 compares this strategy with sending the booth out and back to the Chicago show and then doing the same for the Washington-Baltimore show. Going back and forth each time increases carbon emissions by 72 percent over today's show-to-show routing strategy and incurs a 30 percent price increase over what the exhibitor pays today. Given the 10-plus-year lifespan of the exhibit, out-and-back routing represents substantial financial and eco-penalty.

The exhibitor made greener, and less expensive, routing possible by crating the exhibit. Crates don't fill trailers as efficiently as pad-wrapped exhibits do, so there is an environmental penalty. However, pad wrapping would mean higher storage and drayage costs on a recurring, show-by-show basis and invite the risk of damage. This is speculative, but without crates the environmental gains from improved trucking efficiency might be offset by the environmental and fiscal impacts of frequent repair and replacement. For this exhibitor, the tradeoff wouldn't be worthwhile. For other programs that involve full, dedicated truckloads of properties going to and from many different shows, pad wrapping might be the greener choice. While every trade show program shares the same fundamental economics, each exhibitor's challenges and opportunities are unique, and this is why running the carbon numbers is so helpful.

Figure 5.5 compares two different routing strategies for the hard-wall exhibit. Here's another question: How does shipping the hard-wall exhibit compare to shipping the tension-fabric version with its lower, embodied emissions and fewer crates? Figure 5.6 provides an answer using the exhibitor's current show-to-show routing.

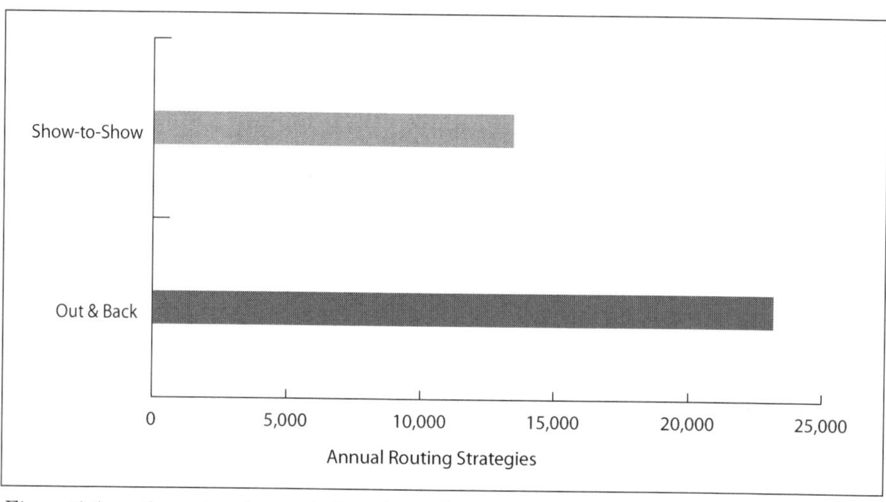

Figure 5.5 — Annual carbon emissions from alternative shipping strategies in pounds of CO_2

In this example, the tension-fabric exhibit reduces transportation emissions by an estimated 54 percent over the hard-wall exhibit, and shipping costs by more than one-quarter. The smaller, lighter packaging also reduces drayage costs on an average per-show basis by almost 40 percent. If you combine these benefits with tension fabric's potential savings on embodied carbon and construction costs, you begin to see how your choice can add up to big gains. By choosing a fabric design in this case, the exhibitor could be enjoying a break on carbon emissions, air pollution, shipping and drayage costs at every show.

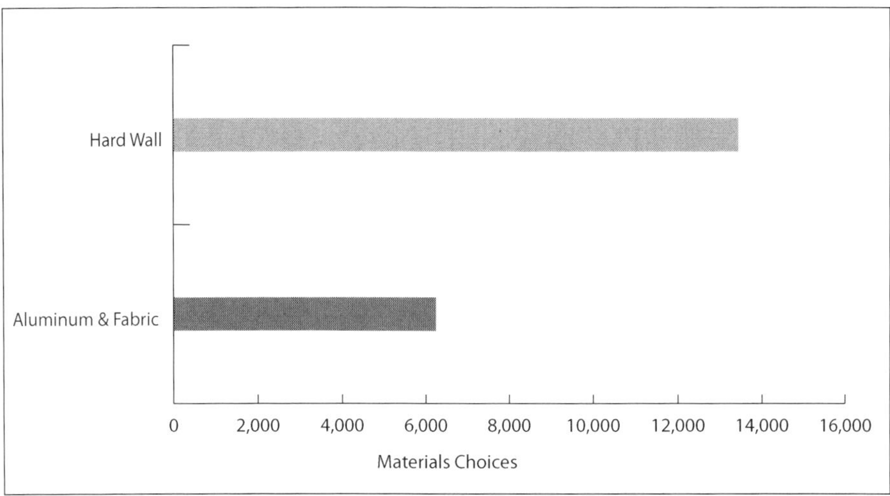

Figure 5.6 — Annual carbon emissions for shipping a hard wall vs. fabric exhibit in pounds of CO_2

One word of caution here: the lesson of this scenario should not be that lighter-weight exhibits reduce carbon emissions per se. The tension fabric exhibit does, indeed, weigh less than hard walls, but it also takes up much less space in the trailer. EPA's emissions factors account for this. As we'll see in the next chapter, size matters more than weight when you ship your booth.

Bottom line: Routing strategies can make a huge difference both financially and environmentally, and if you map routing onto your design and construction planning, the combined benefits can be huge.

Comparing Travel Plans

Deciding who goes to a show, and who stays in the office, is not something exhibit managers can usually get away with. In many companies, attending trade shows seems like a perk, especially when shows are held at attractive destinations. I recall one travel-worn executive telling me that he hoped he'd seen his last Paris Air Show. Meanwhile his less grizzled colleagues were coming up with remarkable ways to explain why their personal, hands-on participation was absolutely vital to the company's future. The same can be said for support staff, regardless of whether they come from the exhibitor or supplier side of the table. During the high-flying 1980s and 90s, it was not unusual for a large exhibitor to manage installations with their exhibit house account executive, the shop owner, a project manager, the lead builder and a variety of audiovisual and lighting techs on site with them. I know—I was one of them, and it was great fun at the time.

The savvy business question is also the Green Edge question here: Are all of these people adding value to your company's investment in the event? Could you do without some of them altogether? In the '80s and '90s the answer was an unqualified yes and everybody knew it, but priorities were different then. Another question is this: Could someone who lives and works closer to the show venue stand in for some of the travelers and be just as effective? The business question is as straightforward as it is familiar: Are you getting a good return on your travel investment?

Applying the Green Edge mantra, *Make Every Decision a Green Decision,™* adds a new dimension to this time-honored query: Is there a more efficient and less destructive way to get the same performance out of the show? I can't answer that question in this case study because it gets to the heart of your company's marketing and sales goals, and how you use trade shows to achieve them. But I can say with absolute confidence that the Green Edge question about staffing a show and the underlying business question are truly one and the same.

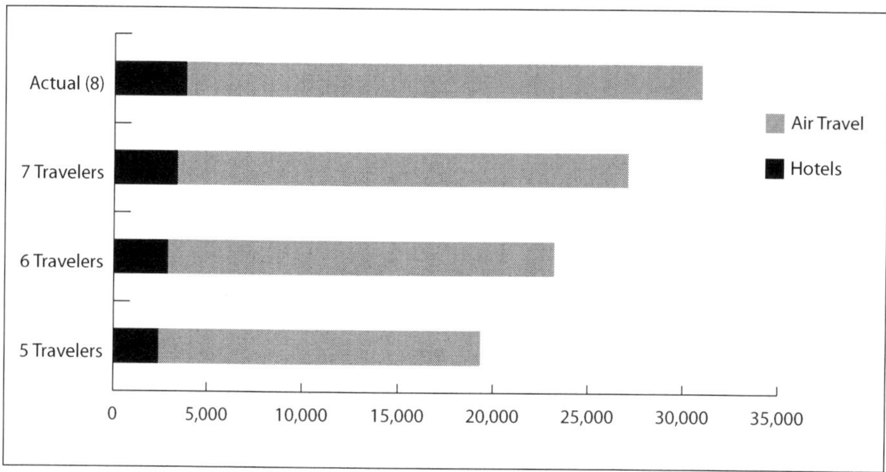

Figure 5.7 — Annual travel emissions (averaged) in pounds of CO_2

When I see more than 100 company staff traveling to and from a large show in order for each of them to attend one or two meetings, I wonder whether the company is being highly strategic or slipping into comfortable patterns that no one really examines. It could go either way because the concentration of customers at trade shows makes these events highly efficient places to make contacts. Trade shows are tremendously intense environments, too, where the competitive pressure to be on hand seems enormous. Sometimes people attend just because they don't want to become conspicuous by their absence. But the highly pressurized nature of shows means they are not always the best places to conduct memorable meetings with customers. The most important question, always, is what's on the customer's mind. There is no point pushing for customer meetings on show site if the customer's head is somewhere else entirely.

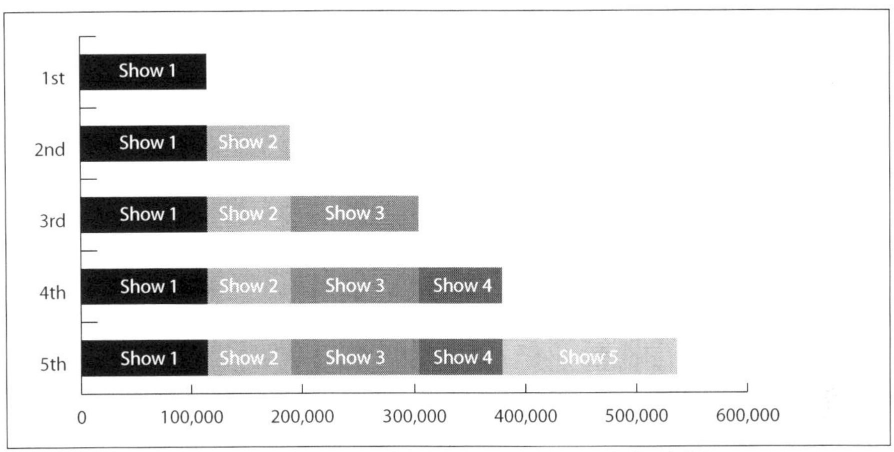

Figure 5.8 — Cumulative travel emissions for five events in pounds of CO_2

For these reasons and because air travel is the most damaging arrow in the quiver, show staffing always deserves a rethink. Even if you can't make the decisions yourself, doing a little carbon analysis will give the ultimate decision-makers a new tool for re-examining whether the company's staffing strategy and corporate culture are working sustainably. Let's take a look.

It's easy to estimate our case study exhibitor's travel footprint by calculating emissions for each round trip flight and hotel stay, and then adding them up. The simplest way to present alternative scenarios to decision makers is to assume that they can eliminate a certain number of people from the total or replace a certain number of travelers with local staff. For convenience, Figure 5.7 compares the exhibitor's current travel formula with one that reduces the total number of travelers in incremental steps. Everything is averaged here, so that you don't have to fret about who gets left at the office. This graph merely reduces the head count, so that decision-makers can start thinking about alternatives.

This case study involves a modest travel program by big show standards; it's nothing like the 100-plus-traveler program described previously. So Figure 5.8 takes a quick look at that larger, more complex situation. It involves an actual five-show series and some realistic assumptions about where all of the travelers live, and how many days each one of them spends on site. Since the shows are in different locations relative to the exhibitor's headquarters and various regional offices, total CO_2 from air travel varies from one show to the next. Figure 5.8 demonstrates how CO_2 emissions accumulate over the five-show sequence.

Sometimes seeing this accumulation of consequences is enough to break the ice. The next step is to figure out how to cut emissions without sacrificing business performance. Chances are good that a company sending more than 100 people to a trade show can wring out the towel without doing any marketing or sales damage. To help facilitate this thought, Figure 5.9 returns to our original case study and presents emissions per point of origin for each show. This way, a decision-maker can see at a glance whether one regional office or another is over-represented and weigh specific personnel versus emissions choices for the shows. Keep in mind that there are different numbers of travelers coming from each location: four from the Southeast, two from New England and one each from the other locations in this scenario. The graph shows their totals by point of origin, but does not show the individual people.

You can imagine what Figure 5.9 will look like for the 100-plus travelers in the larger, five-show scenario. But perhaps this is already enough. Just opening the door and letting the right questions into the room can fulfill the purpose of this exercise. After all, the go-versus-stay decisions will probably be made on the basis of business performance and costs, first and foremost. But with all these numbers on hand you can compare various scenarios fairly easily. It's just a matter of plugging the changes in, tallying the results and asking, "Is this worth the price we're paying?"

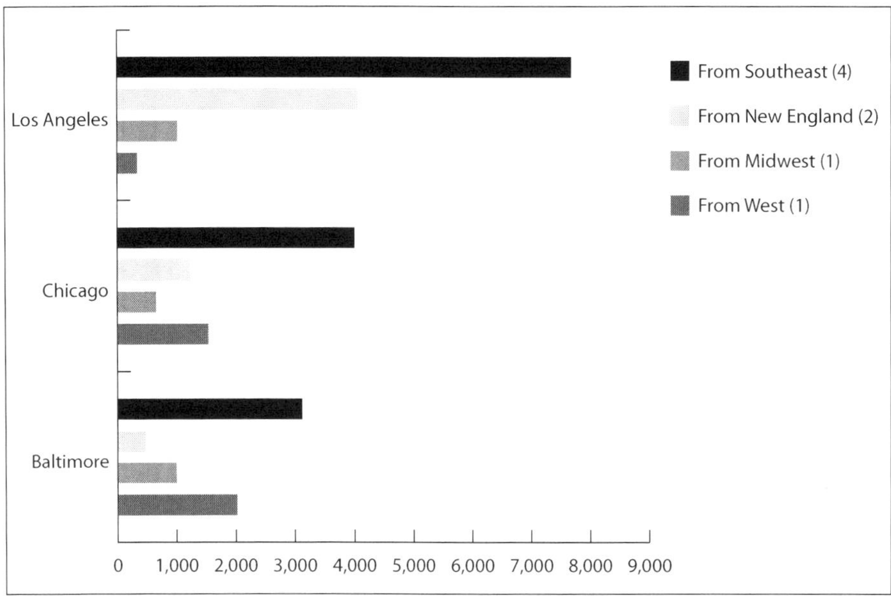

Figure 5.9 — Air travel emissions to each show in pounds of CO_2

If you recall the earlier discussion about my company's decision to reassign supplier visits based on commuting patterns, you know what your company is up against. When people are asked to give up their spaces on the show floor for the sake of fiscal or environmental performance, they will have to find new ways to ensure that their connections to key customers remain strong and productive. This will force them to confront their own versions of the proverbial "Nobody follows up on the show leads!" problem. If they will not be standing in your booth at every show, they will have to find new ways to coordinate with those who are and take the initiative to stay close to their customers. These adjustments don't necessarily come quickly or easily, but with a little time and effort they can succeed.

Bottom line: Business travel represents a big Green Edge opportunity that should never be ignored.

Adding Up the Advantages

Having run comparisons within each of the three major categories of activities it is interesting to see how much of an achievement combining them all might yield. Figure 5.10 presents the exhibitor's actual case study alongside the worst case we identified for out-and-back shipping, and a best-case scenario that uses tension fabric construction and modestly eliminates two travelers to each show. Embodied carbon in the materials is amortized over the 30-show lifespan.

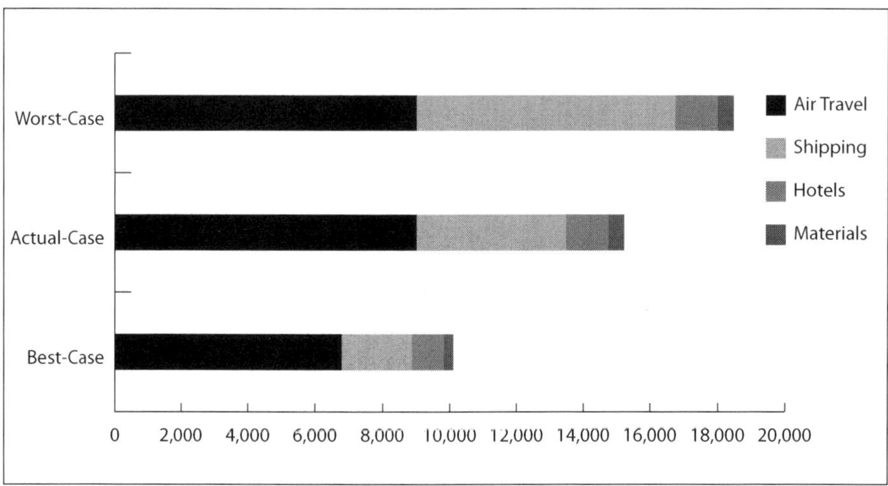

Figure 5.10 — Best-case to worst-case scenarios in pounds of CO_2

In this comparison, the exhibitor's actual activities emit almost 20 percent less CO_2 than the worst-case scenario, but 33 percent more than the best case. Again the caution: These are exploratory estimates that you run in order to discover opportunities. They are not literal emissions, and running additional scenarios might change things quite a bit. But they demonstrate that the program still has room to wring out some waste and reduce recurring costs and carbon emissions, and that the opportunities are large enough to be worth considering.

More importantly, the comparisons within each of the activity categories have served their purpose. We know, for example, that going green is about much more than the booth. Everyone loves to buy and sell green products, and although those products are important, they don't come close to telling the whole story. We've learned that transportation routing and packing strategies can make a very big difference, too, and when you factor transportation into your design and construction planning the benefits of a one-time choice can pay dividends show after show for many years to come.

Nothing else trumps travel, and this is both the greatest opportunity to sharpen your Green Edge and the most vexing problem for exhibit managers. As with everything else, it comes down to balancing business and environmental performance. We've seen enough success stories to know that these two priorities aren't really at odds; and the numbers we've just run prove that they align beautifully around efficiency and competitiveness.

Bottom line: When used as a comparison tool, carbon analysis shines a bright spotlight on some amazing opportunities to cut costs and earn eco-rewards. In the next chapter, we'll take a look at some of your other green choices that carbon metrics don't fully reveal.

Chapter Six

The Green Guide

Let's review what we've learned so far. We discovered that:

- Paying a lot more for one green material might not hurt the bottom line
- A few, simple carbon calculations can reveal big opportunities
- Bigger savings appear when you pool decisions together
- It takes teamwork to pool these resources

Now let's get down to brass tacks with recommendations about when to build, what to build with, how to ship things, what to give to attendees, how to travel, what to serve for hospitality, and how to select and manage a greener supply chain.

Most of the answers are straightforward. But one issue deserves a bit more attention because it confronts the fact that most organizations force managers to work in stovepipes. If you manage the exhibit, someone else manages press events, a third person handles hospitality and one or more other people book the hotel rooms, then you don't control their work and they don't control yours. But if the organization as a whole wants to go green, this looks like a job for teamwork. And that means we need to start with your budget.

Your Budget(s)

One of the biggest "disconnects" in middle management is that dollars aren't really dollars, they're buckets. We often hear our clients say, "I don't really care how much that costs because it's not in my budget." As soon as an organization grows large enough to develop a middle management layer, where various people are responsible for different things, this "stovepipes" problem crops up. Nowhere is the compartmentalization of responsibilities and people more obvious than in the budget.

Or should I say "budgets"? One budget covers major purchases of durable items, such as a new booth, a lighting system or technology for displays. For the most part, accountants will depreciate the value of these purchases on the tax returns over several years. Another budget covers day-to-day expenses, such as refurbishment of your properties, booth space rental, conference registration, transportation, travel and the items you buy that aren't intended to last very long. The accountants will deduct these expenses from the tax bill in just one year. So the United States Congress and the Internal Revenue Service, not your company's executives, are responsible for separating the two biggest buckets that you have to contend with, and the fact that these are separate budgets creates the biggest challenge in your Green Edge planning. We're going to have to solve this.

Then you drill down into smaller buckets, and these could be arranged in any number of different ways. You probably have one bucket for each event, and inside each of these, you'll find all the line items that you manage. In some companies, the exhibit manager has control of all the dollars that fill this bucket. Even though those dollars support a variety of different business units, market segments or product groups, the exhibit management team can apportion spending in ways that serve the company's overall goals and objectives. That's a nice situation to be in because you can manage entire shows, as well as the entire season holistically.

But it doesn't work this way for everyone. In some organizations, the exhibit manager's event bucket gets filled with drips, pours and splashes by managers from other stovepipes who are carrying their own water too. For example, the people who manage a particular group of products might allocate resources to several events that you manage. You might get a drip for one event and a deluge for another, depending on their priorities. In this case, the contributions from all of the different stakeholders, however many there might be, comprise each show budget. This situation makes allocating resources across an entire show season much more difficult.

Of course, some organizations don't really look at show totals at all. In this case, you might be responsible for certain expenses while people in various other stovepipes track other costs that you never see. Do you control the travel budget, for example, or is travel spending handled separately within each of the business units that hound you about registration and hotel room assignments? In this situation, it can be very difficult to manage events in coherent ways because you never get to see the total budgets for any of them.

You see the problem: Nobody has control over everything, and the stovepiping of budgets makes it very difficult to improve overall performance and the bottom line. The solution generally comes down to teamwork. We've already explored how gathering the stakeholders together around a common green purpose will help them understand what you are talking about when you suggest alternative plans. But there is also one special case where a little extra coordination with the folks in the accounting or procurement stovepipe can make a very big difference.

LENGTH OF OWNERSHIP

When we looked at that expensive one-way shipper in the introduction, I mentioned that it might have been built out of furniture-grade plywood. It happens. I've seen it more than once. And it could only happen if the exhibit shop had a stockpile of furniture grade plywood on hand. Nobody is going to rush out to the lumber distributor and buy expensive birch plywood just to build a one-way shipper. From a historical perspective, furniture and cabinet-grade materials have been the mainstays of the traveling exhibition industry for the simple reason that exhibits spend so much of their lives on the road. All that jostling in trucks as they rumble down the highway, all that handling on show sites as the pieces are assembled and disassembled again and again, and all those trips in and out of the storage warehouse are very hard on exhibit properties. If shops used lower-grade materials, your exhibit wouldn't last for more than one or two shows. If you want your exhibit to make it through a season, then it has to be built to take a beating. In addition, the smooth, impressive feel of the exhibit that presents your company's brand image is achieved by using hardwoods, metals and other high-quality materials. Run your hand over a piece of inexpensive construction plywood sometime and imagine what your organization's logo would look like if it were pressed tightly into the undulating wood grain. Most companies would consider this sort of branding a non-starter.

So exhibits are built to last, and the tax code lets your organization deduct the purchase price over five years. There are some exceptions, but that's the basic scheme: The financial value of an exhibit and any of its long-lasting components expires after five years. Most exhibitors are ready for a change by that time too. Marketing messages get stale, the people who staff the booth grow tired of it, and the momentum to create something fresh usually builds up a head of steam by the time the company's capital asset budget shows an allocation for a new exhibit. When this finally happens and it's time to go out to bid on new properties, everyone on your team wants to be involved in imagining the new design. Your exhibit suppliers are chomping at the bit too.

Meanwhile, you continue booking booth space, paying the shipping bills and sifting through invoices for on-site services. I don't need to tell you that these items are part of a different budget; it's the annual expense budget, and all of these costs will be deducted on this year's tax returns. The nice thing about "expensing" things is that you wipe the slate clean at the end of each fiscal year. This clean slate is also where the exhibit house's ongoing costs show up, including all of the labor hours to remove your exhibit from storage, set it up in the shop to make sure it's in good shape, repair anything that's broken and produce those few graphics that will only be used at a few events.

But you already know this. What you might not know is that these two buckets are driving perfectly useful, furniture-grade properties into the landfill long before their time just so they can be replaced by a new set of perfectly useful, furniture-grade properties. In truth, your exhibit walls, display cabinets and crates can easily last 10 or even 15 years. One of our clients built a heavy-duty bolt box in 1986. The word "box" is a misnomer because it's a very large crate-on-wheels that gets filled with all sorts of miscellaneous supplies and small parts. This particular crate has been participating in an extremely active, large-scale event program ever since. It doesn't look terribly attractive after a quarter century of service, but it is still going strong, and its many nicks and stains have become fodder for some amusing exhibit hall lore.

You could say the same thing for many of the company's exhibit properties too. During the 1990s the exhibitor was unable to secure any capital asset money, so the company decided to try to stretch the lifespan of its properties a little bit longer. Since that time they have built many new components, but they still use some of those original wall panels and cabinets to this day. The key to the program's marketing success is that the exhibitor uses its custom parts to reimagine the floor plans frequently, and that the finishes are updated with new colors every few years. The bottom line is that the properties look road worn on the backside that the public never sees, while presenting a beautiful face to event attendees. Competitors even ask the exhibit manager how she can to afford so many new booths and the answer, of course, is that she can't.

The lesson in this story is that exhibits are built to last longer than many exhibitors realize. The exhibitor in our carbon-case study, for example, has been using the same custom exhibit for 10 years. We recently met another exhibitor whose booth is in its 15th year of service and the exhibitor has no plans to replace it. Exhibitors ask me from time to time whether it is greener to keep the properties they already own or build a new booth that's made of greener materials. I know the desire to create something new is always strong, but the answer to this question is to use the booth up before discarding it if you want to conserve natural resources, save energy, limit pollution and cut down on waste.

Is this the whole story? Never: There is always a caveat, and life-cycle ownership is no exception. So the basic Green Edge principle is this: *if using an item or product doesn't consume energy, keep using it for as long as you can.* Since your booth, its cabinets and graphics, your carpet, the hanging sign and other static items can't be plugged into a wall socket, don't throw them away because continuing to use them won't cause any more environmental damage, whereas replacing them will. You are going to have to ship these static properties to shows, of course, which will cause pollution. We'll discuss that issue in a moment, but let's stick with the basic principle a little longer because it will help us understand the whole story.

A second aspect to this Green Edge principle is that *if an item or product consumes energy when you use it, and a new model is more energy efficient than the one you own, you should replace it.* This isn't just a rule of thumb; it's the result of empirical analysis on a wide range of products. Our two Cambridge engineers studied the whole question of when to replace things and came to this conclusion:

> . . . a product with high-embodied energy, low energy in use, and little improvement in use should be replaced less frequently. [In the opposite situation] energy in use is greater than that in production, and efficiency is improving, so the product should be replaced more often.[1]

So static, non-energy consuming properties should be used until they fall apart. Exhibits and crates fit the description perfectly. For items that do consume energy *and where energy efficiency is improving* from year to year—as is the case with video displays, lighting, refrigerators and cars—you should replace them more frequently. LED video displays, for example, use a small fraction of the energy consumed by older plasma TVs, so if you still own a plasma monitor, this guideline would suggest replacing it. New LED TVs are also more efficient than relatively new LCD displays, so always keep electronics on the list of items that you upgrade every few years. The same thing goes for that little apartment-sized refrigerator that you stock with water and sodas in the storage room.

Now let's return to the vexing question of transportation pollution because if you keep the properties you already own, and ship them around the country from show to show your events will be responsible for a lot of air pollution. Here's the thing: If your plan is to replace your exhibit with a new one of similar size, then you will have gained nothing. In this case, the greener choice is to keep the booth you already own and challenge your creative team to reinvent it so that it looks new. If, on the other hand, you plan to replace your booth with a new one that packs into a much smaller footprint, then replacement is the greener choice. The idea, here, is that the new booth will take up less space in the truck, which will make room for other booths so that the total number of trucks belching pollution on the highways can be reduced. There is also a third and more extreme option, which is to eliminate shipping entirely by renting properties locally for each and every event. In this case, there is no question that the greener option is to ditch (i.e., donate, sell or recycle) your old booth and all the air pollution that goes with sending it to shows.

But given the budget bucket dance we started this discussion with, how can you extend the life of your exhibit properties if your choices are being dictated by the depreciation schedule in the tax code? This is where you'll have to rely on teamwork. The goal in tax accounting is to deduct all of an organization's legitimate expenses. If you want to keep your properties for longer than five years, then you're only spending to refresh and replace bits and pieces instead of making a major capital outlay for new construction. The overall costs will be lower, but not zero, and you will still pay the exhibit house to reimagine and refresh your exhibit.

Where are the tax advantages in this decision? Between you, the accountants and your exhibit supplier, you can come up with a simple plan. The exhibit house can separate new items that the accountants want to capitalize from ongoing expenses on future invoices. This is not difficult to do, and you can make reasonable judgments about which line items should be considered capital assets. In our experience, the overall costs will be reduced and mostly allocated to the expense bucket. If you reinvent your old booth en masse, there will be bump in capital spending, of course, but it will be a smaller bump than the cost of a new build. Once that's done, the only capital money you'll need for many years to come will be enough to cover those energy-consuming items that you want to upgrade every so often.

In spite of all the stovepipes, and separate buckets of money, you really can develop a Green Edge procurement plan. It's an accounting and replacement strategy that emphasizes both the financial and environmental benefits of going green.

The Green Edge on Budgets and Replacement

- *Hold on to properties that don't use energy*
- *Hold on to properties that do use energy if efficiency isn't improving*
- *Upgrade properties that use energy if energy efficiency is improving*
- *Upgrade properties to take up a lot less space in shipment*
- *Have your exhibit supplier keep track of capital vs. expense items*

Construction Materials

Which materials are greener than others, and how can you tell you're getting the real deal? Let's go through them one-by-one.

WOOD

The carbon metrics told us how wood compares to other materials, but not whether one piece of wood is more sustainable than another. Fortunately, you can turn to product labels from one of the world's two largest forestry certification programs, the Forest Stewardship Council (FSC) and the Programme for the Endorsement of Forest Certification (PEFC) with its North American endorsees, the American Tree Farm System (ATFS) and the Sustainable Forestry Initiative (SFI). Of these, FSC is considered the most stringent, and it is the only one currently accredited by the LEED rating system for green buildings.

Certified lumber, plywood and paper adhere to a holistic set of principles about long-term forest stewardship and preservation of biodiversity, along with respect for the people and communities that work and live in forests. It's an approach that advances the joint welfare of natural and human communities. These are global programs and they do come under fire from time-to-time for alleged lapses here and there, but they set the standard for sustainable forest products. Foresters, mills, distributors and even exhibit shops need to earn certification to complete a sustainable chain of custody.

The glues used to hold plywood and various forms of hard board together might contain a toxin called urea formaldehyde. But it is possible to buy products that are both certified as sustainable and toxin-free if indoor air quality is a high priority. Look for the term "NAUF," which means "No Added Urea Formaldehyde."

Wood is one area where the green label does cost more. Most exhibit builders use "shop ply," which is sort of like factory seconds. It is a perfectly suitable material, although you won't find it with a sustainable certification. There just isn't enough sustainable plywood to compete at this price point. Costs vary every single day because wood is a global commodity, but on one particular day, one particular distributor quoted sustainable ply as about 30 percent more expensive than domestic shop ply. On that same day the distributor was also offering imported shop ply for about 20 percent less than the domestic variety. Don't take these numbers to the bank, though, because distributors often find special bargains and the price you pay might be quite a bit lower.

Can we do better? Yes, and one reason is that most shops order sustainable lumber only to satisfy a client's request. This means they don't buy enough to get volume discounts. If certified lumber became an exhibit industry mainstay, the pricing would certainly drop.

The Green Edge on Wood

- *Certified lumber helps protect forest ecosystems and communities*
- *It usually costs more, but pricing varies day to day*
- *Volume pricing can bring the costs down*
- *Don't forget NAUF for better air quality*

BAMBOO

Bamboo gets a lot of attention as a sustainable alternative to wood. The main reason is that bamboo, which is a grass, grows incredibly fast. Bamboo can be harvested every five-to-seven-years, whereas it takes decades for hardwood trees to mature. So, the idea is that by utilizing bamboo in construction we can reduce the global demand for hardwood. You can buy FSC-certified sustainable bamboo as well. You might run across some controversy about bamboo processing, most of which involves the chemicals used to turn bamboo stalks into textiles for clothing. These concerns do not apply to the construction trades.

So far, so good, but how would you use bamboo in exhibits? It is an extremely durable material that is ideal for the support frames that you see in some innovative modular systems. It is also used as a flooring material in buildings and as a high-end cabinetmaking material. But its relatively high cost makes it an unlikely choice to replace birch plywood as a mainstay in traditional exhibit construction. In other words, as with tension fabric, switching to bamboo probably means rethinking design in order to utilize its best qualities.

The Green Edge on Bamboo

- *Certified sustainable bamboo is the greener choice*
- *Rethink design to utilize its best qualities in affordable ways*

ALUMINUM AND STEEL

It takes a lot of energy to make both of these metals, yet both can be recycled again and again. In the real world, recycling isn't perfect. For one thing, different alloys of these materials have to be separated before recycling in order to preserve their high quality. Because of this, the often-cited statistic that you can make recycled aluminum for 95 percent less energy than it takes to make "virgin" aluminum is not quite true. In the case of aluminum soda cans, for example, by the time you take all the processing steps into account, a recycled can uses more like 75 percent less energy than one made from virgin stock.[2] That's still quite a big difference in favor of recycling.

But in practical terms your only choice as an exhibitor is whether to use these metals at all because you would be hard pressed to buy aluminum or steel products that didn't already contain some recycled material. Recycling is simply built in. If you plan to take advantage of a metal's long life, and recycle it at the other end, then you are doing all that a consumer can do.

The Green Edge on Metals

- *Recycled material is already built in, so you don't need to hunt for it*

PLASTICS

We use two main types of plastics in exhibits: acrylic and polyvinyl chloride (PVC). The former is more difficult to deal with because there really is no alternative if you want acrylic's glass-like transparency. The main alternative is cast resin, but its relatively high cost and distinctive appearance tend to make it an accent material, not a mainstay. The only way to reduce the amount of pollution associated with acrylic is simply to use less of it.

The same is true of PVC, which is the plastic substrate that is often used for graphic panels. PVC does not decompose readily in landfills, so when you mount your graphic to a sheet of PVC and throw it away after just one or two shows, it will say underground for a very long time. If you already own PVC panels, the greenest choice is to keep using them by mounting new graphics over old graphics for as long as you can. In the future, you can explore alternative substrates, and the number of options is growing every year.

For example, you can buy biodegradable plastic sheets that look and feel very much like PVC. Sheets made from recycled plastic are becoming commonplace, and some of them are biodegradable. Thin, flexible recycled and biodegradable plastic sheets will conform to curved surfaces. For applications where a more rigid material is required, recycled plastic sheets that are faced with aluminum are an alternative to aluminum-faced PVC panels. Non-petroleum-based options include smooth-finished hardboard panels made with FSC-certified wood fibers and non-toxic glues. Hardboards made with various rapidly renewable plant fibers address applications where fiber textures are desired.

Each of these materials—biodegradable, recycled, recyclable and so forth—offers tradeoffs, yet each has a smaller environmental footprint than PVC. The choice of a non-PVC material will depend on the specific application.

The Green Edge on Plastics

- *The greenest alternative to acrylic is simply not to use it*
- *If you own PVC-backed graphic panels, reuse them for as long as possible*
- *Explore PVC alternatives for future graphic panels*

FINISHES

Most exhibits are finished with colorful, high-pressure laminates and virtually all of the brands on the market comply with indoor air-quality standards. Shops, however, have a choice when it comes to the contact cement that they use to glue laminates to plywood. In most of the country, a lacquer-based adhesive is preferred because it dries almost instantly, which speeds production. But lacquer causes air pollution just like oil-based paints do. Water-based contact cement is a viable option and is required under clean-air regulations in some jurisdictions, but the builder has to dedicate some equipment to the process and adjust manufacturing procedures in order to use it.

Paints follow a similar path. In some parts of the country, such as Southern California, air-pollution controls translate into stringent limits on paints that emit unhealthful volatile organic compounds (VOCs). As a result, water-based alternatives are available for everything from wall coverings to automotive finishes. But these restrictions are not nationwide. If cleaner air is your goal, the green choices include water-based paints for metals, plastics and woods.

The Green Edge on Finishes

- *Use low-VOC adhesives for high-pressure laminates*
- *Use low-VOC or no-VOC paints*

FLOORING

The exhibit industry rolls into town on a carpet, and increasingly that carpet contains recycled nylon fibers. Carpet manufacturers use a great deal of recycled nylon because it reduces the need for virgin feedstock. One of the major show contractors made headlines in recent years by announcing a comprehensive recycling program for rental and aisle carpet. Whether you can recycle your old carpet will depend entirely on whether your shop is located near a carpet mill. The end-of-life recycling issue could go either way, but there is absolutely no reason not to select new carpet that contains a high percentage of recycled material.

A new alternative to standard nylon carpet is made from recycled soda and water bottles (PET). Because it is used in food packaging and must be lightweight, flexible and durable, PET is an extremely high-quality plastic. While it's true that plastic degrades every time it is recycled, PET starts at the top of the food chain, so to speak, and recycled PET is a remarkably durable material. Tests by the U.S. National Park Service revealed that recycled PET carpet is more durable, vibrant and resistant to the damaging effects of sunlight than nylon carpet.[3]

An amazing range of green flooring materials might work for you in special applications, such as on decks and stages. These include rapidly renewable materials like bamboo and cork, as well as non-petroleum based linoleum and even recycled rubber mats.

The Green Edge on Flooring

- *Use high-recycled-content nylon and recycled PET carpet*
- *Consider rapidly renewable and recycled materials for special applications*

Graphics

We've already addressed the most important factor in graphics, the substrate material that supports your prints. As noted in the section on plastics, most of these materials, including PVC sheets, PVC-backed aluminum and foam boards can be replaced with recycled, recyclable, biodegradable or non-petroleum based options. Plywood and hardboard substrates can be replaced with FSC-certified equivalents. You can even have logos and images printed directly onto wood and other materials without the need for an intermediate substrate at all. This is a rapidly evolving field with a varied and growing set of alternatives. The selection of greener materials will depend entirely on the application.

For fabric banners you can choose recycled PET, which will deliver vibrant color. A much more subdued alternative is organic cotton cloth, which is usually reserved for special applications where wrinkles and less vibrant color will not be problematic. As for printing processes, the options are so numerous that it pays to work them out with your supplier in order to address your specific needs and concerns.

The Green Edge on Graphics

- *Reuse graphic substrates for as long as possible*
- *Select non-petroleum, biodegradable, recyclable and/or recycled substrates to suit your specific application*
- *Consider direct print on exhibits to eliminate substrates*
- *Consider recycled PET or organic-fiber fabric banners*

Lighting

Just as incandescent light bulbs were phased out nationwide, incandescent show lighting has gone the way of the dinosaur. The most durable and energy-efficient replacement is the light emitting diode or "LED," which uses a small fraction of the energy needed to light an incandescent bulb. LEDs are so efficient because they don't waste very much electricity getting hot, and this means you get light for less energy.

LED lamps offer additional benefits as well. The first is that they last a very long time. The second is that they are virtually unbreakable, and this characteristic makes them especially attractive for our industry. Finally, they are available in a wide range of sizes and styles—enough to suit almost any application. In addition to the screw-in LED bulbs you find at home improvement stores, LEDs are available on strips of tape that can be installed out of sight to create lighting accents and other effects. Larger LED display fixtures can be adjusted to deliver a wide range of colors, ranging from bright, saturated tones to subtle off-white nuances.

Fluorescent lamps—typically two-foot or four-foot long tubes with electronic ballasts—offer a second energy-efficient option for light boxes and other special applications. LED lamps are also available in tubular formats for use in recessed fixtures and light boxes.

The Green Edge on Lighting

- *LED lamps are the most durable and energy efficient*
- *Fluorescent lamps with electronic ballasts are also energy efficient*

Electronics and Appliances

The U.S. Environmental Protection Agency's Energy Star rating system is making appliances more energy efficient year after year. Energy Star is a voluntary program that helps consumers identify the most energy efficient products in a wide range of product categories. Manufacturers submit products that meet EPA's energy efficiency benchmarks. When roughly half of the products in a category meet the standard, the EPA raises the qualification standard for the Energy Star rating. This, in turn, creates a new incentive that pushes manufacturers toward further improvements. In this way, Energy Star keeps driving the marketplace toward greener products. Look for the Energy Star logo on everything from video displays to computer monitors to those back-room refrigerators. If it has an electrical plug, look for the Energy Star logo.

The Green Edge on Electronics and Appliances

- *The Energy Star logo indicates the most energy-efficient options*

Collateral and Premium Items

An exhibitor once asked what she could do to make her collateral materials greener. I suggested that she simply not print any. Think about what you do when you are packing up to head home from a show. Your carry-on bag is bursting with clothes and paperwork already. Now, you have to deal with a pile of brochures and sell sheets that other exhibitors have given you, plus all of the promo cards you received in your registration bag. What do you do with this mess? If you squeeze everything into your luggage so you can read it on the flight home, you deserve a special commendation for your diligence. The knee-jerk reaction is to leave it all behind. You're tired, after all, and you've just completed a very intense experience. Don't you simply want to close the door and move on? Don't you think attendees feel the same way? Many of them do.

If you think there is truth in this vignette, then the costs you pay to print and ship literature to the show should really be amortized across the relatively few copies that are doing your company any good. This scenario makes collateral materials look like a very expensive way to move trees to landfills by way of pulp mills, print shops and shipping firms. Wouldn't it be smarter to have a salesperson follow-up with a prospect after the show ends and people are back at work? "I know they throw it all away," she said. "But my salespeople feel they need to hand something out." Perhaps the greenest thing this exhibitor can do is invest in some sales training.

Logo-emblazoned giveaways face a similar fate in hotel rooms; thus, the question is whether you can come up with something that attendees will actually want keep. I'm sure you have a collection of giveaway items somewhere that you neither look at nor use. Companies are always searching for new items to distribute before the items become fads and everybody suddenly has too many of them. If you need to distribute something, look to one of the companies that source greener choices, and be sensible. The goal isn't simply to put something in a prospect's hand; it's to have the prospect remember you. If your logo-covered, giveaway stays behind in a hotel room, your dollars will have accomplished nothing.

The Green Edge on Collateral and Premium Items

- *Minimizing collateral reduces costs, pollution and waste*
- *Minimizing premiums and selecting useful items also reduces costs, pollution and waste*

Transportation

This is where the lightweight exhibit myth finally dies. It's a simple matter: The truck that hauls your exhibits around outweighs your exhibits, and you would not be able to shave enough weight from the cargo to make a difference. The typical heavy-duty truck is rolling down the road with roughly 20,000 pounds of exhibits onboard. The entire package—tractor, trailer and cargo—weighs closer to 55,000 pounds. Studies have shown that adding or cutting a thousand pounds of cargo has very little impact on fuel economy. In fact, once the truck gets rolling, wind resistance is more important to fuel economy than the weight of its cargo.

The greener move is to pack as many exhibits into as few trucks as possible, and then route those trucks from show to show in ways that minimize the total mileage. Our carbon case study demonstrated how much of a difference these two strategies make.

Beyond this, consider hiring a company that displays the EPA SmartWay logo. SmartWay is a voluntary program for shippers and truckers who run fuel-efficient equipment and adopt efficient routing and no-idling policies. You can find a summary of the environmental benefits on the EPA SmartWay website.[4]

As important as trucking pollution is, it can't hold a candle to the pollution caused by airfreight. As we saw in the carbon-metrics chapter, airfreight produces about five times more carbon emissions per ton-mile than a truck. So, if you book a lot of airfreight, your top green priority might be to avoid last-minute shipments and keep your exhibits, brochures and everything else on the ground.

The Green Edge on Shipping

- *Airfreight creates the most pollution per ton-mile*
- *Routing can reduce truck miles*
- *Consolidating shipments reduces the number of trucks on the road*
- *EPA SmartWay shippers run efficiently*

Travel

We took a close look at airline carbon emissions in the carbon case study. To summarize, air travel is undoubtedly your biggest environmental challenge because conferences, meetings and trade shows are designed to draw people together. This, in fact, is their purpose. Yet, flying creates more environmental damage than just about anything else that you manage.

Can we do better? The options are incremental, but they are also clear. The first priority is to rethink your staffing strategy to ensure that everyone who travels is adding value. Similarly, ask whether people need to travel so frequently in order to attend planning meetings for upcoming events.

Here is a real-world comparison: A new client was preparing a major event in Florida, so they flew our lead designer and account manager from the West Coast to the sunshine state on two separate occasions to survey the venue and review progress on the display. Our people weren't the only travelers since the client flew their own folks in from their headquarters as well. Our team made a third trip for the event itself. The hours they spent together built trust, and the show went off without a hitch. Meanwhile, another far-away exhibitor called us on the phone and eventually hired us, and then worked through a new custom design and construction project without ever asking anyone to travel. Our first face-to-face meeting took place on the show floor in Southern California after the project was complete. In this case, we built trust through the work we did together long distance. In the age of virtual meetings and instant communications, people are saving time and money by doing projects long-distance all the time. So the Green Edge question is, when do we really need to fly?

The second priority, which only applies to short-distance travel, is to decide whether people can carpool or ride trains to the venue. The simple carbon calculations can help you sort out the advantages. The third priority applies whenever flying really is necessary: Go nonstop and minimize connections. The goal is to try not to earn 100k frequent flyer status.

The Green Edge on Travel

- *Virtual meetings and rethinking on-site staffing reduce pollution*
- *Carpools and trains are options for shorter trips*
- *Nonstop flights are the most efficient flights*

On-Site

Choosing green hotels is a matter of reviewing the hotel sustainability statements, and possibly their memberships in some of the voluntary certification programs, such as Green Seal and EcoGreen Hotels. In many cases, selecting hotels that are within walking distance of meeting venues or along mass transit routes might be your greenest option because it will allow you to minimize driving and taxi cab rides.

Inside the event venue, the priorities are simple. The highly visible piles of packing waste in the aisles can be minimized. The objectives are to minimize packing materials, use recycled materials and send them home after the show for reuse and recycling. Eliminating bottled water is always a green choice as well.

The Green Edge On-Site

- *Many hotels publish sustainability reports*
- *Hotels close to event venues and along mass transit routes reduce driving*
- *Recycling and removing packing materials reduces show-floor waste*
- *Minimizing plastic bottles reduces pollution and waste*

Catered Events

Assuming that you have selected green venues and minimized the use of private cars to reach them, your top, green priorities are food choices and how to serve the food. The latter is very simple: Disposable dishware is a high-embodied energy item, regardless of whether it is made of paper or plastic. Reusable china and flatware also embody a lot of energy, but the caterer can reuse them many times, which is the greener choice.

Food is an area that deserves consideration from three different angles: carbon emissions, organic agriculture and toxins. Let's take them in order.

A popular urban myth says that local foods have smaller carbon footprints than foods coming from across the country and overseas. In fact, the worldwide transportation of food accounts for only 11 percent of the total carbon footprint of food.[5] This is because agriculture is an energy-intensive business that utilizes pesticides and herbicides made from fossil fuels, and food processing is also energy intensive. The carbon numbers suggest that if you purchase as many food items as you can from local sources you will probably reduce the carbon footprint of your hors d'oeuvres and meals by only a few percentage points. At the top of the food-carbon spectrum you'll find cattle, which turn out to be energy intensive in their own right. Cattle also generate large amounts of methane producing waste and they exhale methane as well. The results of a major study on the issue suggest that simply eliminating beef and cheese from your next event will do more to reduce its carbon footprint than buying everything you possibly can from local sources. Of course, there are perfectly good social and economic reasons to seek locally produced foods and the carbon footprint metrics do nothing to undermine these values in any way.

A second issue is whether to serve organic foods. While the carbon metrics vary greatly from one crop to another, organic produce is a greener choice.[6] Organic farming allows for more biodiversity along the margins of fields, which can help ecosystems remain resilient in the face of a changing climate and other pressures.

Finally, if you serve seafood, you might want to consider avoiding fish species that are high in mercury and other pollutants. These include tuna, swordfish, sea bass and other large predator fishes. At the other end of the spectrum, species such as cod, salmon, tilapia and shrimp are among a long list of options that are low in mercury. You can find advice on sustainable and low-mercury seafood on various websites.[7]

The Green Edge on Catered Events

- *Reusable service items save energy*
- *Eliminating beef and dairy is the best way to cut carbon*
- *Organic foods help promote resilient ecosystems*
- *Low-mercury and sustainable seafood are more healthful and greener seafood*

Supply Chain

Supply chain management is an essential part of any green business strategy because our companies and organizations rely so heavily on the work that others do on our behalf. This is where, as an exhibitor or meeting manager, you can vote with your pocketbook for a more sustainable industry.

We noted the EPA's SmartWay certification for transportation partners, and the voluntary certification programs that some hotel chains have embraced. But other certification options exist as well, including the APEX/ASTM standard that we will look at in the next chapter. APEX/ASTM offers certification categories that cover virtually every aspect of meeting and trade show support.

If you already enjoy long, productive relationships with your principle suppliers, those relationships and your stretch goals might be enough to encourage your partners to join you in your mission. If you are going out for bids on a new project, then your RFIs and RFPs can set the bar. In this case, you might consider two possible approaches.

The first approach is to ask respondents how they will help you achieve your company's sustainability goals. This approach sets a new relationship off in a green direction from day one. The second approach is to ask respondents to include their own sustainability plans in their submissions. There are no standards for such plans, but there are a few things to look for. First, does the plan address core business operations, or is it limited to providing greener products upon request? Truly, the greenest thing any business can do is clean up its basic operations. Second, does the green business plan provide quantifiable goals and metrics? If a company can show a track record of environmental progress, you can rest assured that its commitment isn't just greenwash. Finally, does the company offer third-party verification of any kind? Here APEX/ASTM certification, reports from The Climate Registry, or other green certifications and memberships will validate a respondent's claims. Since going green is still relatively new to this industry, your efforts can be transformative and they might press suppliers into new areas that they have yet to fully embrace.

The Green Edge on Supply Chains

- *Written sustainability plans demonstrate a commitment to going green*
- *Sustainable operations are fundamental to sustainability*
- *Metrics can demonstrate a track record of progress*
- *Certifications and third-party verification validate performance*

Chapter Seven

Get Certified, Go Public

"Credibility" is now the watchword for corporate social responsibility. Green marketing is no exception. Survey after survey shows that trust in both corporate and government leaders has reached a very low watermark. Gallup's polling, for example, shows a deepening loss of faith in the U.S. Congress, with those who "disapprove of the way Congress is handling its job" hovering in the low-to-mid 80th percentile for most of 2011-2014. Trust in government has never been so low in, at least, the past 40 years.[1] Business struggles to earn the public's trust as well.[2] Wall Street's behavior heading into, and coming out of, the Great Recession demolished people's faith in the things CEOs have to say.

Physicists like to say that nature abhors a vacuum, yet the trust gap facing communication professionals can't be filled in the usual ways. If nobody believes what CEOs are saying, why would people rush to believe the messages churned out by marketing departments? As public relations expert Richard Edleman observed, "Smart businesses will talk to employees first, because citizens now trust one another more than they do established institutions."[3] The don't-worry-they'll-trust-us approach no longer works.

In fact, the Edleman public relations firm's research for its annual Trust Barometer suggests that businesses cannot fill the trust gap without redirecting the focus. As the firm's Neal Flieger explained, "Our analysis shows that the operational factors driving present trust in business aren't enough to expand trust in the future. The path forward requires more of a focus on societal and employee-facing issues."[4]

Recognizing this, businesses are forming partnerships with other organizations that can lend respectability to environmental claims. It's no accident, for example, that Nestlè teamed with Greenpeace—the activist eco-NGO—to solve the company's palm oil image crisis. Nestlè then partnered with two other organizations: the Forest Trust and the Roundtable for Sustainable Palm Oil in order to follow through on the promise to change its ways. The company realized, belatedly perhaps, that it couldn't rebuild consumer confidence on its own. Nor could it rely on a clever marketing campaign. Going it alone would never have rung true with consumers who had already watched the viral Greenpeace-produced video on YouTube—the video that Nestlè had already tried, and failed to squelch. In the end, the company had little choice, but to rethink its supply chain and, ultimately, rely on the credibility of its nonprofit partners to regain people's trust.

The phrase I just used—"in the end"—is really the starting point these days. It is always easier to get on track and stay there than to back up and start over. Because brand loyalty depends on trust more than anything else, businesses are trying to learn the new rules of today's hyper-connected instant-media marketplace. It's a marketplace where business operations are no longer reliably private. Moreover, it's a communications landscape where broadcasting to consumers isn't terribly effective.

Quite a few environmental NGOs are collaborating with businesses in proactive ways to minimize environmental damage. For example, The Nature Conservancy helps wind energy developers avoid building projects in especially vulnerable habitat. As one of The Nature Conservancy's lead scientists, Joe Kiesecker, forthrightly says, "There's no form of energy that doesn't have an impact on our planet. It just depends on the impact."[5] In other words, NGOs and businesses aren't at odds in these relationships. Rather, they are working together because their interests overlap. In a similar way, Greenpeace brought together guitar companies Fender, Gibson, Martin and Taylor to form the Music Wood Coalition. It's an effort to protect tropical forests while also ensuring a future for the guitar industry's most valuable natural resource.[6] Such examples are becoming almost commonplace among companies that are awakening to what Richard Edelman calls the "dispersion of authority in media."[7]

Partnership with an environmental NGO, however, is not the only way to build trust with customers and other stakeholders. A second and very common approach is to report certain types of environmental performance to third-party specialists for independent verification. As GreenBiz.com noted, "Most companies now disclose at least some environmental impacts, and a growing number are having third-party assurance completed on their quantified performance data to make their reporting more credible."[8] Many businesses—even small firms such as mine—report greenhouse gas emissions voluntarily to The Climate Registry, the Global Reporting Initiative or other groups. Using standardized protocols, independent verifiers in turn provide a level of assurance that customers, the media and others are likely to believe. In other words, people don't have to rely on the trustworthiness of businesses alone. They can trust green leaders because independent verifiers are certifying the claims.

All of this makes sense for business communications and marketing in general, but how does it translate to events inside convention centers?

Start by Deciding What You Want to Say

Let's first consider some communication questions that event marketers must contend with. Do you represent a sustainability focused, eco-friendly brand? Are you trying to present a deep, company-wide commitment to sustainability through the design and implementation of the events program? Does the exhibit itself—its materials and construction—need to convey an impression of green leadership? Do on-site presentations—such as graphics, video programs, live performances and face-to-face conversations—need to explain how the company is advancing environmental efficiency across the board? Or, alternatively, is your narrower challenge limited to explaining how management of the events program itself is going green?

Your answers to these questions will help determine how best to proceed. For example, companies with long track records of environmental commitment, such as Keen and Heidelberg, have gained fame with clever, eco-friendly exhibit designs. In Keen's case, an exhibit booth was built almost entirely using discarded shipping pallets. The youthful, outdoor-oriented footwear brand looked right at home in its homage-to-pallets, although you wouldn't expect to see representatives of a financial services company or an engineering firm looking so rough and ready under these conditions. Every brand has its aesthetic limits.

Similarly, Heidelberg utilized discarded objects—used printing plates, in this case—as a cladding material for its largest exhibit in 2012. These two companies applied the same design and construction formula, which was to elevate familiar-but-unwanted objects to the status of image-makers. It's important to remember that in Heidelberg's case, for example, booth design was part of a multi-faceted set of decisions about metrics, transportation logistics, travel, product demonstrations and so on. Still, the similarity of the underlying design philosophies that these two exhibitors employed raises an interesting question, which is whether design alone can convey a sustainability message successfully. Perhaps, but the design and context would both have to be just right. That's a tall order. A visitor to either Keen's or Heidelberg's exhibit could misinterpret the clever reuse of discarded objects as nothing more than a playful twist. Predicting how people will interpret what they see is always problematic, which is why making an explicit statement about environmental performance is also necessary.

Other questions arise too. One is how exhibitors in other markets—where found objects might not be brand-appropriate—should carry the sustainability message to their customers. Do alternative design and construction methods convey eco-performance just as well? Not necessarily: we've already acknowledged that exhibitors are reusing booth properties for many years, yet the colors, finishes and materials themselves do not give this green strategy away. Old properties don't always look old, nor would you want them to. So green marketing must extend beyond booth materials and aesthetics.

Finally, relying entirely on brilliant design doesn't access the trust-building benefits of third-party assurance in a trade show or conference. Regardless of the aesthetic package—whether it includes used objects, bamboo, tension fabric or hard walls—the challenge is to tell a convincing story. This is where the company's partnerships with environmental organizations, reporting to third-party verifiers and good storytelling come into play. If green business is central to the brand proposition, then devoting a certain amount of graphic or video real estate to a company-wide sustainability story might make sense. If, on the other hand, your assignment is to acknowledge the improving eco-efficiency of your event program itself, then a more restrained strategy is probably required. In other words, you can figure out how to tell an engaging story about green business or rely on third-party certifications to tell it for you.

Green Is a Journey, Not a Destination

If you study how eco-brand leaders explain their sustainability programs you will quickly discover some invaluable lessons.[9] First, green leaders never claim that they have achieved sustainability. They have not "gone green." Leaders recognize that their companies are still doing a certain amount of environmental damage no matter how much they have achieved, so they talk about efforts that are evolving over time. It's crucial to acknowledge the process itself because consumers are justifiably wary of ostentatious claims. Admitting that the company is working on a long-term project also conveys the all-important quality of humility. We are all in this together.

Second, green leaders recognize and admit that they don't have all the answers. In 2007, when sustainability was first catching on in the event industry, a cohort of exhibitors, suppliers and event organizers generated a great deal of passion and vitality by sharing ideas and information with one another. Each organization was trying to improve, but none of them was holding out on their peers. Meanwhile, a number of other folks kept what they learned close to the vest. One of them told me that he didn't want to sacrifice his competitive advantage. The trouble with this attitude, as we now know, is that consumers view sustainability as an ethos, not a marketing claim. Going green is an effort to raise the standards of practice for everyone. If we aren't willing to teach and learn from one another, we're breaking an essential, if unwritten, rule of sustainability.

Third, green leaders understand that credibility develops over time. Conversely, it can be squandered in an instant. Because the desire to announce breakthroughs is overwhelming, you see it expressed in statements such as, "We cut waste by 10,000 tons." The numbers are almost always impressive, but remember that Chevrolet improved the Tahoe SUV's fuel economy by 25 percent with hybrid drive. Isolated facts invite scrutiny, and the outcome of close inspection can be unkind. This is why green leaders anchor factoids with graphs or statements showing incremental progress—and setbacks—over the years. It's the trend, not the isolated number that earns respect.

Fourth, green leaders understand that we're in a "trust, but verify" world. They anchor sustainability report cards with verified metrics. It's true that you can't verify everything, but if you verify a few important things, you lend legitimacy to other results. For example, our firm reports energy use to The Climate Registry. The results show a lasting two-thirds reduction in carbon emissions relative to our 2006 baseline. My company also keeps track of landfill waste, recycling, employee driving, water use and—to some extent—employee commuting. None of these latter categories are included in The Climate Registry's reporting protocol, so our progress on them is not verified by anyone other than us. We call this out when we make a progress report available to the public. A cynic could say there is no way to be sure that our self-reported results are accurate. That's true, but psychology doesn't really work that way. Companies invest in third-party verification because it demonstrates a commitment to integrity that everyone assumes applies to the entire green enterprise.

Finally, green leaders tell their stories from the heart—and from the beginning. Leaders present the mission and goals—including stretch goals—and what remains, yet to be done. Trusted brands are not shy about their social and environmental commitments, nor do they hide from the challenges they face living up to them.

Building credibility for your eco-commitment and achievements involves three basic principles that are easy to follow. The first step is to *tell us about your motivation*. Lead with the company's commitment to its environmental focus. In a time when trust of public leaders is so low, your primary mission is to demonstrate that the business wants more than financial returns alone. If your company cares about people, ecosystems, health or the next generation, don't bury the lead below the fold.

Second, *give us a story, not a list of facts*. Random facts and figures quickly become disorienting. Too much data can make people suspicious that something sinister is hiding under the spreadsheet. If you say, for example, that you cut landfill waste by 10,000 pounds, you beg the question of just how much waste the company is generating. Every fact and figure needs some context, such as a trend over time or a comparison between here and there. Keep the comparisons simple so that people can understand them at a glance. For example, "We started here, we've come this far, and you can see how much farther we still have to go."

Lastly, *it's never about you*. The company is undoubtedly working with outside partners on some or all of its green initiatives. Tell us who they are. They might be your principle suppliers, nongovernmental organizations, civic groups, employees or local volunteers. People are looking for evidence that your company means what it says about its social commitments. As Edelman's Neal Flieger noted, "The path forward requires more of a focus on societal and employee-facing issues." Prove that you are walking the talk.

Third-party verification of your efforts to go green will validate the company's claims. For companies that are reluctant to devote a great deal of real estate to the sustainability story, a certifier's logo provides a shortcut. Finding validation for green event management was not possible until recently, but this is no longer the case.

Get Certified

"Certified Green" would be a terrific label to display next to your company logo or in a report to the company's executives. Let's consider three ways to pursue this Holy Grail.

GREENBUILD MANDATORY EXHIBITOR GREEN GUIDELINES (GMEGG)

Although it isn't an industry-wide certification, the first model comes from the U.S. Green Building Council (USGBC). The USGBC is the organization behind the voluntary Leadership in Energy and Environmental Design (LEED) rating system for green buildings. As part of their education and advocacy work, the organization stages an annual show and conference called the Greenbuild International Conference and Expo. Greenbuild was the first large conference in the United States to define and implement mandatory environmental performance standards for exhibitors. Phased in over several years, the standards began with a pledge, giving exhibitors time to learn the ropes, before finally becoming obligatory.[10]

Greenbuild's strategy involves specific performance benchmarks for energy use, materials reuse and disposal, transportation, packaging waste, air pollution and more. Because show organizers understand that exhibitors might approach the requirements in different ways, each regulation provides two or three compliance options. For example, in addition to replacing all incandescent lamps with energy-efficient lighting, the exhibitor must also do one of the following: either reuse all booth lighting or upgrade to new LED lights for general lighting and T12 fluorescent tubes with magnetic ballasts in light boxes. In this example, the least energy-efficient lamps (incandescent) are banned outright. In addition, each exhibitor is free to choose between reusing relatively efficient lights or replacing them with new, even more energy efficient equipment. By offering this choice, GMEGG codifies the when-to-upgrade strategy described in the "Length of Ownership" section of the last chapter.

Looking past light bulbs, GMEGG applies the same strategy to other electronics. Exhibitors are prohibited from bringing single-use exhibits to the show. They are encouraged to select recycled construction and printing materials, minimize brochures and giveaways, and donate unwanted properties to community partners. In addition, exhibitors are required to choose logistics and transportation suppliers that participate in the EPA SmartWay Partnership Program. In this way, Greenbuild incorporates an existing high-quality, third-party certification into its program. Greenbuild and its exhibitors benefit from the SmartWay standard without having to reinvent the wheel, so to speak.

Every show organizer faces a host of challenges, not the least of which is competing to attract exhibitors and attendees. In a highly competitive marketplace, mandatory performance standards might seem like barriers, yet the success of Greenbuild's conference proves that green requirements can be implemented successfully. Your company might not work in the building industry, in which case you won't be a Greenbuild exhibitor. This show, nevertheless, sets the standard for organizer-driven eco-performance. Adopting these standards is one way to say—without third-party verification, of course—that your events program is compliant with a cutting-edge performance standard that was developed by a highly respected institution.

APEX/ASTM SUSTAINABLE MEETINGS STANDARDS

In 2011, the Convention Industry Council's Accepted Practices Exchange (APEX) and ASTM International, which is a nonprofit organization that is accredited by the American National Standards Institute (ANSI), published the APEX/ASTM Environmentally Sustainable Meeting Standards.[11] The standards grew in partnership with the Green Meetings Industry Council (GMIC) and the EPA. The goal was to establish a consistent and coherent approach to eco-efficient events from top to bottom. When an event organizer becomes APEX/

ASTM-certified, the requirements extend down the supply chain to all of the organizer's suppliers, including venues, accommodations, general contractor, marketing communications providers, caterers, transportation suppliers, audiovisual companies—every entity that participates at the overall event planning level.

APEX/ASTM also includes standards for exhibits, which means that exhibitors and their principle suppliers can also be certified. Certification is granted through an auditing process. The Green Meetings Industry Council, which administers the program, has designated iCompli, a division of the third-party assurance provider BPA Worldwide as the auditor for APEX/ASTM applications.

Like the GMEGG, the standards are performance-based. Unlike GMEGG, this is a tiered system, in which the broadest range of requirements is addressed at the entry level. Requirements become increasingly stringent as a candidate advances through levels two, three and four, but only in a few categories. APEX/ASTM focuses primarily on environmental performance by way of benchmarks for waste management, energy conservation, air quality, water conservation and supply chain management. Additionally, an applicant is required to submit a written staff management plan that designates at least one person to lead the company's environmental efforts. Partnership with community organizations is required for the purpose of donating discarded properties in order to minimize landfill waste.

Many of the performance standards mirror the Greenbuild requirements. As with GMEGG, you are likely to find the APEX/ASTM benchmarks well within reach. For example, the level one standard for electrical equipment requires that 25 percent of all electrical equipment (appliances and electronics) shall be energy efficient. In another category, EPA SmartWay shippers will be used at least 20 percent of the time. As you can see, the standards apply to the exhibitor's entire show schedule rather than a single event. This makes compliance relatively easy by granting the exhibitor a great deal of flexibility.

The track record of other voluntary, performance-based standards—such as the LEED rating for buildings, for example—suggests adoption will gradually ramp up across the industry. Certified exhibitors can display their status at trade shows and enjoy the respectability of uniform, industry-wide standards and an audited certification process. Moreover, as you will see in the appendix—The Green Edge Matrix—the recommendations that are offered throughout this book will prepare you for a certification process.

ISO 20121 EVENT MANAGEMENT SYSTEM

An Environmental Management System (EMS) is a different animal from the approaches we've considered so far. Termed "specifications" rather than checklists, International Organization of Standards (ISO) requirements are intended to encompass all of the elements of an effective management system. As a result, an ISO specification outlines a process for identifying environmental impacts, designing and implementing responses, measuring performance and adapting for continual improvement.

The ISO developed ISO 20121 based on an earlier British event management standard (BS 8901).[12] As the numerical name implies, the specification was published in 2012 and it was first used at the 2012 London Olympics. ISO specification takes a triple bottom line approach to sustainability, which requires attention to economic, environmental and social impacts of event management. Since the specification provides no performance benchmarks, the exhibitor develops them through a rigorous process of stakeholder engagement, analysis, scope definition and so forth.

Figure 7.1—The ISO 20121 event management process

In practice, the process need not be as daunting as it might sound. After all, you probably know who your primary stakeholders are: your principle suppliers, internal and external customers and the communities in which you do business. You can't simply follow your hunches, however, and remain ISO-compliant. Instead, ISO mandates a transparent and documented process involving a series of specific steps. In shorthand, those steps define a circular pattern of constant improvement: plan, do, check, act, plan, do, check, act and so on. To expand on this a little, the exhibitor must define the scope of the challenge; identify the relevant stakeholders; define the environmental, economic and social issues; develop an action plan to address the largest negative impacts; establish objectives; monitor performance; and make improvements.

Moreover, the company's overall sustainability goals can help to define the objectives for the event team's ISO 20121 program. The goals and plan, however, must ultimately be responsive to stakeholders' interests. This makes the EMS much more targeted on impact remediation than APEX/ASTM or the GMEGG. Additionally, ISO 20121 was developed to be compliant with ISO 1400-based Environmental Management Systems that many companies use. ISO 20121 provides a pathway for integration of events into a larger corporate EMS. Since the ISO 14001 family of standards involves facilities, process management and Life-Cycle Assessment, there has never before been an effective way to bring event management into the EMS.

The nature of a specification, as opposed to performance benchmarks, makes the ISO EMS much more flexible and attentive to the company's stakeholder concerns. On the other hand, the due diligence requirements are high.

ASSEMBLING THE PUZZLE

Both APEX/ASTM and ISO 20121 were developed to capture all of the issues relevant to the organizer of a trade show, conference, sporting event, concert, festival or any other type of large-scale gathering. As an exhibitor, you are one of many entities that the event organizer must engage. Your perspective is naturally more narrowly focused on the issues that are under your control. But you might consider thinking about your annual schedule less as a collection of isolated events than as one long event. I've made the case that zooming out will reveal opportunities that are invisible when you are working on details. You need to back out to see the proverbial forest for the trees. From this larger perspective you will discover opportunities to pool resources and engage your suppliers in cleaner, greener events year-round.

Let's return to the problem of demonstrating green performance on the show floor. If your communication objective is limited to management of the events program itself, less could be more. A small plaque indicating APEX/ASTM certification, ISO 20121 EMS compliance or measurement by a third-party organization might do the trick. As noted earlier, third-party logos are shorthand for credibility. A small plaque near the reception counter might say, in effect "APEX/ASTEM level-one certified sustainable event management."

Chances are, however, opening the conversation with such a plaque will lead to further questions that you should be prepared to address. Whether you address them with a more expansive graphic story or a short video presentation in your booth, or direct visitors to a sustainability web page will depend on your audiences. Every market is different. At the Natural Products Expo West, for example, visitors might be eager to engage in conversations about sustainable event management. The natural products industry is an eco-friendly market, after all. On the other hand, audiences at the National Space Symposium or the Sea-Air-Space Exposition might have other concerns on their minds. In the latter case, a third-party certification or verification logo could be sufficient. Exhibitors at "Expo West" should be prepared to take visitors on a longer walk. Either way, the basic rules of green marketing apply: Tell people why you care, put facts and figures in context and demonstrate that your company is engaged with other partners in its green journey.

DON'T FORGET YOUR PEERS

This discussion brings us to a final point: The greening of the meetings and events industry will be driven largely by peer pressure and competition. This is how innovation always spreads: When a few pioneers demonstrate the benefits of doing something new, others begin taking notice. A novelty becomes a trend, which eventually becomes business as usual. We are seeing this evolution begin in various corners of the industry already. For example, a great many exhibitors have abandoned printed collateral materials in favor of electronic brochures or follow-up efforts to prospective customers. The industry still has a long way to go.

Breaking the ice is the other reason to go public. By stamping your on-site presence with a certification logo, a green award logo or a simple graphic representation of your company's commitment and progress, you are helping to shape our collective expectations. You are saying that sustainability matters to your company, which means that it should matter to other companies as well. While you should never underestimate the power of a press release, you should, likewise, never underestimate the reason your company invests in live marketing in the first place. When people see their competitors doing something new, they pay attention.

Chapter Eight

What Does Going Green Mean?

If doomsday predictions about the future leave you wondering whether to cancel next season's event schedule altogether, take a deep breath. People have been gathering in marketplaces around the world since the dawn of civilization. In some cities, you still find bazaars on the same sites where people have been buying and selling for hundreds of years. So cutting live meetings off at the knees seems impractical at best. In fact, a survey by the Center for Exhibition Industry Research showed that business gatherings are financially efficient: Companies spend nearly five times more to identify a potential customer, and get the first meeting, without a trade show lead to open the door.[1] Whether this number is high, low or right on the money makes little difference because organizations find value in meetings. Why else would your company spend so much time and money on them?

Rather than throw the baby out with the proverbial bathwater, let's figure out how to preserve the benefits of face-to-face gatherings while minimizing the harmful side effects. It's good business to do so, and it's a good way to move the industry forward.

You might already know how the United Nations World Commission on Environment and Development defined "sustainable development" a quarter-century ago: "*Sustainable development is development that meets the needs of the present without compromising the ability of future generations to meet their own needs.*"[2] No doubt your job description has a narrower mission than the UN's effort to end poverty, but you might agree with a strategy that combines cost-effective business today with a healthy respect for those who will eventually take your place. One of the challenges, of course, is distinguishing between the organization's genuine needs and mere extravagance, and this question evokes many different points of view. Although this book can't give you a simple answer, there's no escaping the fact that as soon as we talk about corporate social responsibility and making decisions that affect other people, we're really talking about ethics and obligations.

Ethics and the Green Edge

I'll be the first to admit that it would be very unusual to write a book about going green if I didn't think we ought to do so. To be clear, it seems to me that we have neither the capacity nor the right to prevent people in the developing world from enjoying higher standards of living. As they advance, the inevitable consequences of increased consumption and waste will exact a hefty price unless we take concrete action. This is why I set out to reduce my company's environmental footprint, and asked third parties to verify its progress. If we move quickly to clear some space—environmentally speaking—for those who are just now coming into their own, we'll do our part to slow the progress of environmental change. We'll also buy some time for greener technologies, cleaner energy sources and more sustainable ways of doing business to come online.

Ultimately, sustainability will require much more than the inspired actions of a few green pioneers, but these examples show the way. Like the Wall Street investors who are betting on sustainable brands, I think backing the Green Edge is a businesslike no-brainer and the ethical choice as well. I agree with Yvon Chouinard about using our businesses to help solve the environmental crisis, and I sincerely doubt that I would have done the research for this book if I didn't think so.

Having said that, I also know that larger, publically traded companies and cultural institutions deal with complex pressures and demands that privately owned businesses don't contend with. For them—and quite possibly for you—going green involves different tradeoffs, as well as compromises that middle managers rarely have the power to control. I get it: Even if you want your events program to be as green as it can possibly be, your efforts might be constrained by outside forces. I also understand that you might see things very differently than I do. The simple truth is that the future will be what humanity creates collectively and not what any one of us might want.

As I said before, this book doesn't make a moral argument about how green your events program should be or which issues your company should embrace. But I find it very helpful to know something about the arguments that other groups use to make their cases. Knowing where stakeholders are coming from is invaluable when your mission is to build trust and respect for your brand. It can help you foresee and prepare for new costs or restrictions that might be coming your way as well.

Much of environmental law seems to revolve around two ethical precepts. One is the "Precautionary Principle," which states that if an act is thought to be harmful, but there is room for doubt, the burden of proof falls on those who want to take the action. In simple terms, if burning a lot of fuel might have a negative impact on farmers and the world's poorest people, for example, those who want to burn the fuel are supposed to refrain unless they can prove that their actions won't cause any harm. In reality, we burn fuel every day of our lives, and perhaps because everyone does it, no government or court is forcing us to stop. Even so, many dedicated people are working to change this in various says. The cap-and-trade systems in California, New England and Europe, for example, are gradually raising the price of fossil fuel pollution in order to spur restraint and low-carbon innovation.

The second precept is that when the time comes to clean up an environmental mess, the polluter is supposed to pay the bill. Consequently, do industrialized nations or businesses owe financial support or carbon allowances to developing nations? While finding the answer probably isn't on your to-do list, the question itself is influencing corporate behavior. It's certainly one of the reasons why companies are eager to demonstrate their commitments to sustainability and build trust with outside stakeholders. In recognition that trade shows are front-line expressions of their brands, companies such as Heidelberg and Hewlett Packard are ensuring that event managers reflect these commitments.

A geopolitical force is also in play behind these precepts; in a resource-constrained world, where access to fresh water, minerals and the right to pollute is at a premium, some sort of allocation process might evolve. The various cap-and-trade systems and California's low-carbon-fuels standard are attempts to limit access through statutory limits and higher costs.

Whether such systems catch on elsewhere remains to be seen, but market forces might eventually have the same effect.

Finally, environmental justice is a top priority for some communities and NGOs. The central question is whether certain groups of people are paying an unfair price in terms of pollution, poverty, poor health and urban blight for the sake of everyone else. Environmental justice finds expression, for example, in forestry certification programs that embrace the welfare of communities that supply forest products.

These various moral dimensions of sustainability help explain why outside stakeholders are pressuring companies and other institutions to embrace sustainability, along with other aspects of corporate social responsibility.

So What Does "Going Green" Really Mean?

Geopolitics, ethics, finance, certification and corporate social responsibility—this book would be pretty useless if it didn't provide a simpler way to think about sustainability. Here it is: "green" and "sustainable" are synonymous with "environmentally efficient." The concept of environmental efficiency boils down to doing your job with as light an environmental touch as you can. An extremely green approach would:

- *Use as little energy as possible*
- *Use as few materials as possible*
- *Use materials as thoroughly and for as long as possible*
- *Emit as little toxic and carbon pollution as possible*
- *Create as little waste as possible*

So far so good: We've encountered these concepts repeatedly throughout this book. Each of them helps limit some type of environmental harm. Yet given what we know about the challenges facing natural ecosystems, wouldn't it be useful to expand our definition to include something more proactive, such as promoting the resilience of forests, agricultural lands, waterways, fisheries, migration routes and other natural systems? After all, resilient ecosystems will be better able to cope with environmental change. So we might expand our "as little as possible" list to include making decisions that:

- *Enhance the resilience of nature*

Finally, since many people share concerns about environmental justice, wouldn't it also make sense to enhance the well-being of those who provide materials and labor to our programs? Companies that buy from local suppliers think this way. So we might expand our "as little as possible" and "natural resilience" list to include making choices that:

- *Improve the well-being of the people who support our programs*

This seems pretty simple: Use very little, waste very little, don't make a mess, strengthen nature and don't take advantage of the people who help you.

Marketing and Extravagance

Since waste reduction is the key feature of so many green business programs, let's take a look at what waste reduction means. As everyone knows, waste is the unwanted material that ends up in landfills and other dumping grounds. Waste is also the unusable by-product of our work, including the air pollution and other environmental damage that comes with extracting and refining raw materials. Measuring the embodied energy and embodied carbon of products and materials helps define this problem.

Waste also refers to using things extravagantly, carelessly or without purpose. Extravagance deserves a little more attention because marketing and other creative industries have never really embraced this issue before.

During the boom times of the 1980s and 1990s, extravagance was a sign of success and market leadership. Exhibitors would frequently fly exotic, hard-to-get materials from distant factories to their exhibit houses in the nick of time for the sake of polishing their brand presentations. Booths were often clad in heavy, fragile materials, such as marble tiles, which were extremely expensive to maintain. Shipping carpets, fabrics and other materials overseas via airfreight was not out of the question either, when designers and exhibitors weren't satisfied with the options they could find in country. On more than one occasion, companies even flew large, custom exhibits to international shows. In addition to the enormous airfreight bills, the carbon pollution from these exercises was in the hundreds of thousands of pounds per flight. As I witnessed all of these things, I also saw high-quality, custom properties head to the landfill after being used only once. The attitude among many exhibitors, and exhibit house account executives, was to create something big, bold and new each and every time out. People simply weren't thinking about the environmental consequences of their choices in those days.

It's hard to imagine making those same choices today. They were symptoms of a high-flying economy and a marketplace that measured leadership by its opulence. Yet it is equally hard to imagine our industry restraining itself if and when such good times return. The competitive urge for one-upmanship is just too strong. Of course, environmental and economic conditions will have a lot to say about the future of extravagance in our industry. The drive in recent years has been to cut costs and cut them again. So this might be the ideal moment to learn something new: how to be both financially and environmentally efficient as we deliver exceptional, highly competitive live presentations.

I wonder what our next few choices will look like in 20 years.

Conclusion

Today and Tomorrow

We've come a long way. We learned that going green is good for business. You can improve the eco-performance of your meetings or trade show program without sacrificing your company's business objectives. On the contrary, lower costs and better environmental performance go hand-in-hand.

We learned that going green is fairly easy: just follow the recommendations in the Green Guide. These will put your meetings or events program on solid ground, where you won't be buffeted by urban myths or greenwashing.

We learned that going green is good for brands. You can bolster your company's reputation with a forthright statement about your goals and with honest progress reports. APEX/ASTM certification will provide the reassurance of third-party endorsement. In a more formal way, ISO 20121 will open a pathway for participation in a corporate-wide environmental management program under the ISO 14000 family of standards.

We learned that you could act today. The Green Guide recommendations address choices that you make in the normal course of doing business, so there is no need to wait. That's the beauty of the Green Edge mantra: *Make Every Decision a Green Decision.*™ Because the recommendations are easy to understand, they will get you moving quickly along the path toward sustainability.

We learned that setting goals will sharpen your focus, and that seemingly impossible stretch goals will spur innovation faster than you might have thought possible. Achieving very large financial and environmental co-benefits requires teamwork. Stretch goals encourage everyone to reach across organizational stovepipes and supply chains to reinvent procedures in more eco-efficient and cost-effective ways.

You can put these insights to work on your own. You don't have to wait for budget approval or permission: just begin making greener decisions. When you do rally the troops around a common stretch goal, however, the collective energy and collaboration will accelerate your progress.

That's the Green Edge in a nutshell. It's available to you right now.

What Comes Next?

We've also explored some of the global forces and social pressures that are driving businesses to embrace sustainability as part of CSR. Will these forces transform the meetings and events industry? Nobody can say for sure. "Tomorrow" is a notoriously unreliable commodity, and innovations will derail punditry every time. Nevertheless, looking into the near future might get the creative juices flowing, and creativity is what going green is all about.

One thing is clear: Nothing has yet derailed the human desire to gather for education, networking and commerce. Despite considerable hand wringing, neither the Internet nor social media nor even economic hard times have killed the meetings and events industry. If anything, technological innovations generate new activity, and cost-cutting drives innovation. Outside forces nudge the industry in ways that people both love and hate, but they don't displaced the basic drive to meet face-to-face.

This doesn't mean trade shows and conferences won't change. In fact, with rising costs and concerns about environmental damage, the industry will almost certainly evolve. We are, after all, a highly creative group of people. In a rapidly moving world, the last thing creative professionals are likely to do is sit still. So what might the future of events and meetings look like?

For one thing, because waste is costly, we probably need to get more life out of the materials we use. So imagine a stretch goal: *own next to nothing*. Is this even possible? What if builders produced fewer solid structures? After all, exhibits are nothing more than portable facades. Tension-fabric, pop-up exhibits and framework systems span open spaces with insubstantial materials. Could we push this idea further? Already, building engineers are using detailed structural analysis to cut down on the amount of material used in beams, floors and walls.[1] Adding strength by adding material has had its day. Can you imagine using highly engineered, low mass structures on the show floor? Zooming out farther, is building facades really the point? Does creating brand expressions require ownership of anything at all? How might creative people—both designers and entrepreneurs—rethink such questions?

On a related topic, shipping is a large part of the event industry's environmental footprint. Imagine another stretch goal: *ship next to nothing*. Could we do such a thing? Efficient routing and consolidated packaging address the problem incrementally. Is it possible to work with a trusted supplier to create a branded environment at each of your events without transporting a custom booth to any of them? Is it possible to rethink which parts of a presentation make each exhibitor unique?

Air travel is even more costly to the environment than shipping. Imagine a third stretch goal: *fly next to nowhere*. Could we still stage events? Europeans mount extremely large trade fairs every two-to-four years rather than annually. Can you imagine concentrating your marketing and educational resources around a different type of event schedule? Is it possible to imagine combining shows with other business travel into less frequent, but much larger activities?

Finally, have you considered whether events are your company's biggest problem? How many times have you heard that sales organizations ignore trade show leads? All the potential cost- and eco-efficiency go up in smoke every time this happens. Imagine a final stretch goal: *follow up on every lead*. Is it pie-in-the-sky to think this could happen? The environment doesn't know whether the extra tons of pollution come out of your stovepipe or the stovepipe down the hall. Can you imagine the sales force becoming genuinely invested in the outcome of events?

In the end, sustainability is rooted in business fundamentals: getting the most out of every dollar—and every pound of pollution—spent. That's the Green Edge.

Let's Move

Each of the stretch goals I just proposed is designed to get you thinking in far-reaching ways. Ultimately, through the event industry's inherent creative energy, we will push one another toward ever-more sustainable trade shows, conferences and corporate meetings. This book gets you in on the ground floor, which is both exciting—and filled with opportunities—and, perhaps, a bit daunting. As I said at the outset, the Green Edge is double-edged. Green business is a cutting-edge enterprise. The cutting edge is where businesses find competitive advantages, yet the cutting edge also gives rise to confusing claims and counterclaims, both honest and disingenuous. This book provides stability to meeting and event planners seeking reliable guidance in a turbulent new business environment.

The other edge—the competitive edge—is where the most successful businesses and other organizations shine. Throughout this book the Big Ideas have nudged you toward this way of thinking. *Be bold. Do the Impossible.* Those who are willing to rethink everything from the ground up will find themselves reaping surprising rewards. This has been my experience: Going green brought lower costs, greater enthusiasm, stronger customer loyalty and a better reputation to our firm. It can be your experience too.

If you think sustainability is a passing fad, think again. Going green isn't like a budget-cutting exercise, in which you trim the fat around the edges and defer large purchases until the good times roll once again. Going green is more like turning a page—it's a page you will never want to turn back. The new, greener page will mean lower costs and invigorated organizations.

Who would not want those benefits? Whichever model you embrace—whether straightforward guidance or flights of creative inspiration—your green actions will pay dividends to your company and our world. You will make progress—*we* will make progress—either way, as long as you give the Green Edge a try. What could possibly be more exciting than that?

Appendix

The Green Edge Matrix

	Performance Recommendations and Standards			Management System
Item	**The Green Guide**	**Greenbuild (GMEGG)**	**APEX/ASTM**	**ISO 20121**
PRIORITIES	(1) Environmental & health (2) Social responsibility (3) Financial success	(1) Environmental & health (2) Social responsibility	(1) Environmental & health (2) Social responsibility	(1) Environmental & health (2) Social responsibility (3) Financial success
BACKGROUND	Developed from best available data on environmental impacts and costs from respected institutions, government agencies and scientific organizations as recommendations to exhibitors, meeting managers and industry suppliers.	Developed by the U.S. Green Building Council (USGBC) as mandatory exhibitor standards for the Greenbuild International Conference and Expo. The GMEGG specifies performance benchmarks.	Created by the Convention Industry Council's Accepted Practices Exchange initiative (APEX) and the international standards organization ASTM International in 2012. As custodian, the Green Meetings Industry Council (GMIC) certifies applications using iCompli audits. APEX/ASTM specifies performance benchmarks. *Numbers (below) refer to Level 1 specifications.*	Developed by the International Organization for Standardization (ISO), based on an earlier British Standard (BS 8901) for event management. First used at the 2012 London Olympics. ISO specifices management practices but no performance benchmarks. *Numbers in "()" refer to the iCompli certification form.*
WRITTEN PLAN	Write a sustainability plan.	Submit a written sustainability policy.	Level 1 (4.3.1.1): Write a sustainability plan.	(2) Determine the scope (e.g., one event or event program). (4) Develop a written plan to address stakeholder concerns.
GOALS AND METRICS	Use stretch goals with clear targets, specific deadlines, quantitative metrics.	Submit goals and objectives as part of the sustainability policy; and complete an online exhibitor survey collection information about booth design, construction and operations.	Compliance with performance standards for the desired level (1–4).	A transparent process for defining objectives based on your goals and stakeholder concerns. (3) Determine key issues for each interested party (e.g., waste, traffic, noise, pollution, GHGs, local resources, animal welfare, sustainable foods). (5) Set "SMART" objectives: Specific, Measurable, Achievable, Reasonable, Time-bound.

	Performance Recommendations and Standards			Management System
Item	**The Green Guide**	**Greenbuild (GMEGG)**	**APEX/ASTM**	**ISO 20121**
RESPONSIBLE PARTY	Designate one or more staff members to implement the plan.	Exhibit manager or event coordinator.	Level 1 (4.3.1.2): Designate one or more staff members to implement the plan.	(1) Buy the ISO standard and identify a responsible party.
MONITORING	Do-it-yourself audits and supplier reports.	On-site audits of 10% of exhibitors.	Audits are conducted during the certification process.	(6) Monitoring procedures required.
VERIFICATION	Highly recommended where appropriate for your goals (e.g., carbon metrics).	Submit compliance information in advance of the show. Greenbuild also conducts random on-site audits.	Apply for certification GMIC and through iCompli.	Demonstrate voluntary conformity by either: first party self-declaration, second party confirmation by interested parties (e.g., clients and suppliers), or accredited third party certification.
REUSE AND LENGTH OF OWNERSHIP	Extend the life of properties beyond the 5-year depreciation schedule. Upgrade energy-consuming items more frequently if energy efficiency is improving over time.	No single-use exhibits are allowed. Reuse booth flooring, signage, counters and paneling. Reuse lighting and electronics or upgrade to improve energy efficiency.		
SHARED OWNERSHIP	*Better:* Rent or lease properties in event cities. *Good:* Rent properties that are shipped to events.			
ACCOUNTING AND TAXES	Track capital verses expense costs for tax deductions on reused properties.			
END OF LIFE	*Best:* Sell, donate or contribute to custom rental intentory. *Good:* Recycle discarded properties.	Donate to other organizations.	Level 1 (4.3.8.1): Partner with community organizations to reuse or repurpose surplus materials left from events that cannot otherwise be reused.	

	Performance Recommendations and Standards			Management System
Item	**The Green Guide**	**Greenbuild (GMEGG)**	**APEX/ASTM**	**ISO 20121**
MATERIALS USAGE REPORT	Request from your suppliers.	Written report documenting all booth construction materials.		
POP-UP DISPLAYS	*Better:* Reuse existing displays. *Good:* When necessary, replace with high recycled and recyclable content. *Good:* When necessary, replace with high recycled and recyclable content.	At least one of the following: reuse existing display, new display are 100% recyclable, or new display is 25% recycled content.		
WOOD PRODUCTS	Choose certified sustainable lumber and plywood or bamboo.			
PAPER	Choose certified sustainable, high recycled content.	Minimum recycled content: 25% for signage, 100% for collateral.		
METALS	Most aluminum and steel include recycled content. Recycle at end of life.			
ACRYLIC	*Better:* Eliminate (e.g., choose cast resin). *Good:* Reduce the quantity used.			
HIGH PRESSURE LAMINATE (HPL)	Virtually all HPL complies with low-VOC standards.			(5) Air quality is to be considered.

	Performance Recommendations and Standards			Management System
Item	**The Green Guide**	**Greenbuild (GMEGG)**	**APEX/ASTM**	**ISO 20121**
ADHESIVES	Choose low-VOC or zero-VOC glues.	One or more of the following: no glues are used to maintain reused properties or glues are low- or zero-VOC.		(5) Air quality is to be considered.
PAINTS AND VARNISHES	Choose low- or zero-VOC coatings.	One or more of the following: no paint/varnish are used to maintain reused properties or paints and varnishes are low- or zero-VOC.		(5) Air quality is to be considered.
CARPET	*Better:* Reuse existing carpet. *Good:* High recycle content nylon or recycled PET, as well as low- or zero-VOC.	One or more of the following: No flooring or use flooring for one year or new flooring is either 25% post-consumer recycled or 100% recyclable or rapidly renewable; flooring is certified non- or low-VOC.		(5) Air quality is to be considered.
OTHER FLOORING	Choose recycled rubber, linoleum, certified sustainable bamboo or other rapidly renewable materials.	One or more of the following: None or use for one year; new flooring is 25% post consumer recycled and 100% recyclable; non- or low-VOC.		(5) Air quality is to be considered.
GRAPHIC SUBSTRATES	*Better:* Reuse existing substrates. *Good:* Choose from a variety of non-petroleum or recycled, recyclable and, biodegradable substrates or direct print onto properties.	One or more of the following: None or reused for one year or new graphics are 100% recyclable or contain 25%+ recycled content.	Level 2: Use graphics that meet at least two criteria: rapidly renewable resource, post-consumer content, low enviornmental impact materials, bio-derived or vegetable-based inks, UV inks, can be repurposed or recycled or both.	
GRAPHIC FABRICS	Choose recycled PET or organic fiber fabrics.			
GRAPHIC PRINTING	Print using water- or vegetable-based inks.	Print using water- or vegetable-based inks.		

Performance Recommendations and Standards				Management System
Item	**The Green Guide**	**Greenbuild (GMEGG)**	**APEX/ASTM**	**ISO 20121**
ELECTRICAL EQUIPMENT	Choose Energy Star rated products.		Level 1 (4.3.4.2): 25%+ of all electrical equipment is energy efficient. Level 2: 50% Level 3: 75% Level 4: 90%	(5) Air quality is to be considered.
ELECTRONIC DISPLAYS	*Better:* Choose Energy Star rated displays, LED displays. *Good:* Choose LCD displays.	Reuse from previous events or upgrade to Energy Star efficiency.	Level 1 (4.3.4.2): 25%+ of all electrical equipment is energy efficient. Level 2: 50% Level 3: 75% Level 4: 90%	(5) Air quality is to be considered.
LIGHTING IN BOOTH	Choose LED lighting for most applications and high-efficiency fluorescent for special applications.	Replace all screw-base bulbs with high efficiency (LED or CFL). In addition, reuse lighting or upgrade to LED with high efficiency fluorescent as needed for backlit displays.		(5) Energy use is to be considered.
OVERHEAD LIGHTING	Choose LED or other high efficiency lighting.	Use high efficiency lighting.		
WATER FEATURES	Use water reclamation systems (pumps and holding tanks).	Use water reclamation systems (pumps and holding tanks).	Level 1 (4.3.6.1): Use water reclamation systems (pumps and holding tanks).	(5) Water use is to be considered.
COLLATERAL MATERIALS	*Better:* Eliminate by using e-brochures or customer follow-up meetings. *Good:* Choose post-consumer recycled paper, certified sustainable paper, non-petroleum inks; reduce quantities.	100% recycled and recyclable paper, plus one or more of the following: eliminate promotional literature or limit to 2,500 handouts and giveaways combined or printed on 50%+ post-recycled material or on 30% recycled material certified as sustainably sourced by a third party organization.	Level 1 (4.3.3.2): Limit the number distributed at the event. Level 2: Distribute promotional materials via electronic delivery and samples on a limited basis.	(5) Waste use is to be considered.

Performance Recommendations and Standards				Management System
Item	**The Green Guide**	**Greenbuild (GMEGG)**	**APEX/ASTM**	**ISO 20121**
PROMOTIONAL ITEMS	*Better:* Eliminate. *Good:* Distribute a limited quantity of useful items made from recycled and/or rapidly renewable or biodegradable materials.	One or more of the following: Eliminate or limit to 2,500 giveaways and handouts combined or 30%+ post-consumer recycled content or rapidly renewable or biodegradable.	Level 1 (4.3.3.2): Limit the number distributed at the event. Level 1 (4.3.8.2): Donate surplus samples (food and non-food) that cannot otherwise be reused by the exhibitor.	(5) Waste is to be considered.
PROMOTING PARTICIPATION	*Better:* Use electronic media rather than printed announcements and invitations. *Good:* Use 100% post-consumer recycled paper and bio- or vegetable-based inks; limit the number to the minimum requirement.		Level 2: Use electronic methods of promoting exhibition participation.	(5) Waste is to be considered.
CLOTHING	Choose organic and natural fibers.			
AIRFREIGHT	Eliminate or minimize air shipments.			(5) Air quality and energy use are to be considered.
TRUCKING	Choose EPA SmartWay or equivalent shipper, pack as densely as possible, route show-to-show rather than out and back wherever possible. Eliminate one-way shipping crates. Minimize packing materials and use recycled or biodegradable materials.	EPA Smartway or equivalent shipper, plus one or more of the following: no materials shipped or polystyrine (packing peanuts) eliminated or all padding and crates will be reused or shipments will be consolidated or crates will be made from a third-party-certified sustianable material or exhibitor will purchase carbon offsets to cover all shipping to and from Greenbuild.	Level 1 (4.3.5.1): 20%+ use of EPA SmartWay shippers (or similar government-verified and approved program that reduces fuel consumption for all trucks and rail, and reduction of emissions of CO2, NOx and SOx, particulate matter and air toxins). Level 2 (A3.6.1.1): 40%+ Level 3 (A3.6.2.1): 60%+ Level 4 (A3.6.3.1): 80%+"	

Performance Recommendations and Standards				Management System
Item	**The Green Guide**	**Greenbuild (GMEGG)**	**APEX/ASTM**	**ISO 20121**
ROUTING	Plan shipping and packing options to minimize miles. Use show-to-show routing and in-route storage between shows whenever possible.			
PACKING STRATEGY	Minimize volume during shipments to reduce the total number of trucks on the road; minimize single-use shipping containers and padding; choose reusable, recycled and/or biodegradable packing materials; pack out what you pack in.			
BOOTH AND SUPPORT STAFF	*Better:* Minimize traveling personnel by utilizing local resources (sales reps, technical staff, hosts, suppliers) and electronic meetings whenever possible. *Good:* Consolidate events with other business trips; fly nonstop.		Level 2: 25% of additional personnel from local sources. Level 3: 50% of additional personnel from local sources, plus exhibitor-appointed contractors and local labor union labor must sign an adherence notice of sustainability policy and practices as applicable. Level 4: 75% of additional personnel from local sources.	
SHORT-HAUL TRAVEL (<300 MILES)	*Best:* Minimize trips. *Better:* Carpool in a fuel efficient car or bus. *Good:* Use a train or bus, carpool in an average car or fly nonstop.			
MEDIUM- AND LONG-HAUL TRAVEL (>300 MILES)	*Best:* Minimize trips. *Better:* Ride trains whenever possible. *Good:* Fly nonstop.			

	Performance Recommendations and Standards			Management System
Item	**The Green Guide**	**Greenbuild (GMEGG)**	**APEX/ASTM**	**ISO 20121**
ON-SITE TRANSIT	*Best:* Walk or use show shuttles or mass transit. *Good:* Carpool in fuel efficient cars or taxi cabs.			
HOTELS	*Better:* Choose hotels with sustainability policies within walking distance of events or public transportation or show shuttle stops. *Good:* Choose hotels with sustainability policies.			
TRADE SHOW TRASH	Eliminate single-use packaging, crates and padding materials; pack it in/pack it out; remove broken boxes of literature; do not abandon booths in place.	Shipping requirement includes options for eliminating polystyrine (packing peanuts) or all padding and crates will be reused.	Level 1 (4.3.3.1) Pack-in/pack-out policy: divert all possible waste into available recycling streams and pack-out the rest.	(5) Waste is to be considered.
ON-SITE ELECTRIC POWER	Plug everything into power strips and turn them off at the close of the show each night (except to protect perishable goods); turn all booth lighting off at the close of each night.		Level 1 (4.3.4.1) Turn off electronic equipment at the close of each night unless perishable goods are at risk. Level 2: Unplug all electronic equipment at the close of each night unless perishable goods are at risk.	(5) Energy use is to be considered.
HOSPITALITY VENUES	Choose venues with sustainability policies; minimize private transportation to events.			
FOOD CHOICES	*Better:* Eliminate red meat and cheese (the two most carbon-intensive foods) *Good:* Select organic food, sustainable and low-mercury seafood. Support local growers and food producers.			

	Performance Recommendations and Standards			Management System
Item	**The Green Guide**	**Greenbuild (GMEGG)**	**APEX/ASTM**	**ISO 20121**
FOOD WASTE	Donate surplus to community partners wherever possible.		Level 1 (4.3.8.1): Donate surplus samples that cannot otherwise be reused to community partners.	(5) Waste is to be considered.
FOOD SERVICE	*Better:* Eliminate disposable service items and beverage bottles. *Good:* Choose compostable and non-petroleum plastic service wear.			
PRINCIPAL SUPPLIERS	Include sustainability criteria in RFPs. Request written sustainability plans describing sustainability improvements to operations (not only products). Request third-party verification, memberships and green awards. Select firms with sustainability certifications such as APEX/ASTM, ISO 20121, SmartWay and others.		Level 1 (4.3.7.1): Establish criteria for purchasing environmentally preferrable products. Level 1 (4.3.7.2): Minimize packaging associated with all purchases and show incremental progress, annual goals and results. Level 3: Florist meets at least one of the following: plant reclamation, replanting, and in-house composting. Level 3: Florist addresses fair trade, local and organic requirements that align with 20%+ of environmental policies and objectives. Level 3: Exhibitor-appointed contractors and local union labor sign adherence notice of sustainability policy and practices. Level 4: Purchase 20%+ event materials from local sources.	(5) Include sustainability criteria in RFPs. ISO 20121 is relevant to all members of the event industry supply chain including organizers, event managers, stand builders, caterers and logistics suppliers.

Performance Recommendations and Standards				Management System
Item	**The Green Guide**	**Greenbuild (GMEGG)**	**APEX/ASTM**	**ISO 20121**
CARBON OFFSETS	Consider carbon offsets ("RECs") for carbon emissions from travel, transportation and exhibit materials. Consider choosing offset partners that meet your social development goals as well.	Exhibitors may purchase carbon offsets to meet the optional portion of the shipping requirement.		
COMMUNICATE TO SUPPLIERS	Promote teamwork by presenting your plan to principal suppliers.		Level 2: Communicate sustainability policy to stakeholders, staff and attendees. Level 2: Communicate purchasing criteria to vendors and encourage them to meet the criteria.	(5) Communications and community engagement are to be considered. See item (3) below.
COMMUNICATE RESULTS TO STAKEHOLDERS (Executives, Certifiers, Others)	Prepare progress reports comparing results to past performance and goals; include any third-party verification and supplier certification; outline next steps; include responses from partners and stakeholders.		Level 2: Provide empirically verifiable documentation to support environmental claims; communicate the sustainability policy to stakeholders, staff and attendees; provide event planners and others with a document detailing environmental policy and practices. Level 3: Accurately represent appropriate environmental initiatives in external communications to key stakeholders and document the ways in which key stakeholders and attendees can support or add to the environmental initiatives.	(3) Identify stakeholders who might be affected by your activities: attendees, employees, volunteers, media, suppliers, investors/sponsors, other exhibitors, civil society organizations, government officials and regulators, local community(s).
COMMUNICATE RESULTS TO INDUSTRY PEERS	Contribute your success stories, strategies, solutions and barriers to help others go green.			(5) Communications and community engagement are to be considered. See item (3) above.
RECOGNITION	Awards and recognition build momentum in communities and across the industry.	Greenbuild offers the Greenbuild Green Exhibitor Award.		(5) Communications and community engagement are to be considered. See item (3) above.

Notes

Introduction

1 Joel Makower, *State of Green Business 2013* (GreenBiz Group, 2013), 6, http://info.greenbiz.com/rs/greenbizgroup/images/state-green-business-2013.pdf?mkt_tok=3RkMMJWWfF9wsRonv6%2FKZKXonjHpfsX%2F7%2BsIT%2Frn28M3109ad%2BrmPBy%2B3IEIWp8na%2BqWCgseOrQ8kl0JV86%2FRc0RrKA%3D.

2 Wayne Cunningham, "Chevy Tahoe Hybrid Wins Green Car of the Year Award," *C/net*, November 15, 2007, http://reviews.cnet.com/8301-13746_7-9818120-48.html.

3 U.S. Environmental Protection Agency, *Green Vehicle Guide*, http://www.epa.gov/greenvehicles/Index.do;jsessionid=yQTqSp3TW0djjh197LTzf7S91vf0J1c1kwBd6nGDNNNvxQT3120p!1789104575.

4 Travis Stanton, "As a Matter of Fact," *Exhibitor*, June 2008, http://www.exhibitoronline.com/exhibitormagazine/june08/editorial0608.asp#.Ut75K6Wtu2w.

5 Read a summary of this issue in Tom Bowman, "Ask Mr. Green: We Are Considering Buying Lightweight Exhibits to Make them More Sustainable," Exhibitor, December 2013, http://www.exhibitoronline.com/topics/article.asp?ID=1517&catID=101#.Ut8izKWtu2w. Various reports reach this conclusion about the impact of payload weight on fuel economy in heavy-duty trucks. See National Research Council, *Technologies and Approaches to Reducing the Fuel Consumption of Medium- and Heavy-Duty Vehicles* (Washington, DC: The National Academies Press, 2101. See also American Transportation Research Institute, *Estimating Truck-Related Consumption and Emissions in Maine: A Comparative Analysis for a 6-axile, 100,000 Pound Vehicle Configuration* (Agusta: Department of Transportation, 2009), http://www.maine.gov/mdot/ofbs/documents/pdf/atrimainereport.pdf. See also Michael Ogburn, Laurie Ramroth and Amory B. Lovins, *Transformational Trucks: Determining the Energy Efficiency Limits of a Class-8 Tractor-Trailer* (Boulder: Rocky Mountain Institute, 2008), http://www.rmi.org/Knowledge-Center/Library/T08-08_TransformationalTrucksEnergyEfficiency. See also Northeast States Center for a Clean Air Future, *Reducing Heavy-Duty Long Haul Combination Truck Fuel Consumption and CO_2 Emissions* (Boston: NESCCAF, 2009) http://www.nesccaf.org/documents/reducing-heavy-duty-long-haul-combination-truck-fuel-consumption-and-co2-emissions.

6 Julian M. Allwood and Jonathan M. Cullen, *Sustainable Materials with Both Eyes Open* (Cambridge, England: UTI), 11.

7 Christopher L. Weber and H. Scott Matthews, "Food-Miles and the Relative Climate Impacts of Food Choices in the United State," *Environmental Science and Technology*, 42. No. 10 (2008): 3508-3513, http://psufoodscience.typepad.com/psu_food_science/files/es702969f.pdf.

8 Paul A. Griffen and Yuan Sun, "Going Green: Market Reaction to CSR Newswire Releases," *Social Science Research Network*, January 29, 2012, http://ssrn.com/abstract=1995132.

9 Daniel C. Esty and Andrew S. Winston, *Green to Gold: How Smart Companies Use Environmental Strategy to Innovate, Create Value, and Build Competitive Advantage* (New Haven: Yale University Press), 244.
10 Convention Industry Council, *The Economic Significance of Meetings to the U.S. Economy: Executive Summary*, February 2012.
11 Convention Industry Council, *The Economic Significance.*

Chapter One: How to Use This Book

1 Charles Pappas, "HP's Lean, Green Exhibit Machine," *Exhibitor*, December 2013, http://www.exhibitoronline.com/topics/article.asp?ID=306&catID=37#.UvfMGaWnnD8.
2 Lena Valentry, "Trash talk," *Exhibitor*, 2010. http://www.exhibitoronline.com/topics/article.asp?ID=1242&catID=71#.UuBn_6Wtu2w.
3 Allwood and Cullen, *Sustainable Materials*, 11.

Chapter Two: How Green Is Green?

1 GreenBiz Forum 2013, "Yvon Chouinard: Why There Is No Kinship between Apple and Patagonia," *GreenBiz Group*, http://info.greenbiz.com/SOGB2014Download_ThankYou.html?alild=48675010.
2 Fair Labor Association, "Patagonia," http://www.fairlabor.org/affiliate/patagonia.
3 Patagonia, *FAQs*, http://www.patagonia.com/us/patagonia.go?assetid=67517.
4 Yvon Chouinard, "On Corporate Responsibility for Planet Earth," *Patagonia*, http://www.patagonia.com/us/patagonia.go?assetid=2386.
5 Griffen and Sun, "Going Green: Market Reaction," 1.
6 Makower, *State of Green Business 2013*, 5.
7 Greenpeace, "Ask Nestlè CEO to Stop Buying Palm Oil from Destroyed Rainforest," *YouTube.com*, https://www.youtube.com/watch?v=1BCA8dQfGi0.
8 Arlene Ionescu-Somers and Albrecht Enders, "How Nestle Dealt with a Social Media Campaign Against It," Financial Times, December 3, 2012, http://www.ft.com/intl/cms/s/0/90dbff8a-3aea-11e2-b3f0-00144feabdc0.html#axzz2rL5pX2IA.
9 Pappas, "HP's Lean, Green Exhibit Machine," *Exhibitor*, 2008. http://www.exhibitoronline.com/topics/article.asp?ID=306&catID=37#.UvfMGaWnnD8.
10 Charles Pappas, "Heidelbert's Green Exhibit Machine."
11 Daniel Cusick, "Awareness of Climate Costs, Risks Builds among Major Companies—Survey," *ClimateWire*, January 22, 2014, http://www.eenews.net/climatewire/2014/01/22/stories/1059993249.
12 U.S. Census Bureau (website), *State and County QuickFacts*, http://quickfacts.census.gov/qfd/states/00000.html.
13 Attwood and Cullen, *Sustainable Materials* 66.
14 The *Climate Report*™ podcast presents a wide range of expert views on issues in business, science, the arts and society. See Tom Bowman, "How Could Our World Change Suddenly? With Richard Alley," *Climate Report*, January 25, 2014, http://tombowman.com/posts/how-could-our-world-change-suddenly-with-richard-alley/. See also Richard B. Alley, *Earth: The Operators' Manual* (New York: W. W. Norton, 2011).
15 Tom Bowman, "How Can Vineyards Survive the Changing Climate? With Lee Hannah and Steve Matthiasson," *Climate Report*, April 27, 2013, http://tombowman.com/posts/how-can-vineyards-survive-the-changing-climate-with-lee-hannah-and-steve-matthiasson/. See also the original scientific paper: Lee Hannah, Patrick R. Roehrdanz, Makihiko Ikegami, Anderson V. Shepard, M. Rebecca Shaw, Gary Tabor, Lu Zhi, Pablo A. Marquet and Robert J. Hijmans, "Climate Change, Wine and Conservation," *Proceedings of the National Academy of Sciences of the United States of America*, 110, no. 17 (2013): 6907-6912, http://www.pnas.org/content/early/2013/04/03/1210127110.full.pdf+html.

16 Tom Bowman, "How Can Vineyards Survive."

17 National Research Council, *Informing Decisions in a Changing Climate* (Washington, DC: The National Academies Press, 2009), 1.

18 National Research Council, *Informing Decisions*, 1.

19 The threshold is an increase in the global average surface temperature of 2°C above the average prior to the Industrial Revolution. Selecting this particular target was a policy choice adopted by the nearly all nations under the U.N. Framework Convention on Climate Change (UNFCCC). The choice was made on the basis of scientific evidence showing that an 80% reduction in greenhouse gas emission by mid-century gives a 3-in-4 chance of limiting global warming below the 2°C threshold. See U.N. Framework Convention on Climate Change, "Milestones on the road to 2012: The Cancun Agreements," *United Nations*, 2012, https://unfccc.int/key_steps/cancun_agreements/items/6132.php.

20 Crusick, "Awareness of Climate Costs."

21 Tom Bowman, "Are Businesses Still Earning an Eco-Advantage? With Andrew Winston," *Climate Report*, February 2, 2013, http://tombowman.com/posts/are-businesses-still-earning-an-eco-advantage/.

Chapter Three: How to Go Green

1 Esty and Winston, *Green to Gold*, 209.

2 Esty and Winston, *Green to Gold*, 209.

3 Esty and Winston, *Green to Gold*, 209.

4 The Climate Registry, which is an independent, non-profit verification organization, verifies Bowman Design Group's greenhouse gas emissions annually. The verification covers so-called Scope 1 and Scope 2 emissions, and the company measures progress against a baseline year, 2006. See http://www.theclimateregistry.org.

5 David J. C. MacKay, *Sustainable Energy: Without Hot Air—Ten-Page Synopsis*, (Cambridge: UIT, 2008), 3, http://withouthotair.com/synopsis10.pdf.

6 Southern California Edison, "The Elusive Enemies of Efficiency in the Home," *Energy Vampires*, https://www.scehomeenergyadvisor.com/learn/vampire.

7 Esty and Winston, *Green to Gold*, 209.

Chapter Four: The Amazing Carbon Metric

1 Carbon dioxide (CO_2) dominates most of the measurements that are of interest to meeting and event managers, mainly because it is the most abundant greenhouse gas that transportation and construction activities emit by a wide margin. Other greenhouse gases, such as methane, nitrous oxide, chlorofluorocarbons and others are emitted in much smaller amounts. The term "carbon dioxide equivalent" (CO_2e) is a way of simplifying the longer list of greenhouse gases into an equivalent amount of CO_2. For our purposes the differences between CO_2 and CO_2e numbers are no more than one or two percent, which is well within the margins of error. You are liable to see both numbers used throughout this book simply because the various information sources only give one or the other.

2 The Union of Concerned Scientists, *Cooler Smarter: Practical Steps for Low-Carbon Living* (Washington, DC: Island Press, 2012), p. 75

3 For tailpipe emissions from gasoline and diesel fuels, see U.S. Environmental Protection Agency, *Greenhouse Gas Emissions from a Typical Passenger Vehicle*, EPA-420-F-11-041 (Washington, DC: EPA, 2011), http://www.epa.gov/otaq/climate/documents/420f11041.pdf. Combining this information with vehicle miles-per-gallon information on the EPA's *Green Vehicle Guide* website is a handy way to compare vehicle choices. If you want to compare various modes of transportation and travel, a widely used resource is the EPA's guidance for voluntary reporting under the Climate Leaders Program. See U.S. Environmental Protection Agency, *Optional Emissions from Commuting, Business Travel and Product Transport: Climate Leaders Greenhouse Gas Inventory Protocol Core Module Guidance*, EPA430-R-08-006 (Washington, DC: EPA, 2008), http://www.epa.gov/climateleadership/documents/resources/commute_travel_product.pdf.

4 U.S. Environmental Protection Agency, *Greenhouse Gas Emissions from a Typical Passenger Vehicle* gives these values in metric terms: 8,887 grams of CO_2 per gallon for gasoline and 10,180 grams of CO_2 per gallon for diesel.

5 The Union of Concerned Scientists, *Cooler Smarter*, 53.

6 U.S. Environmental Protection Agency, *Green Vehicle Guide*

7 U.S. Environmental Protection Agency, *Green Vehicle Guide*

8 CarbonFund.org and TerraPass.com are two websites with air travel calculators. CarbonFund.org offers the option of calculating RF. See CarbonFund.org, "Reduce Your Individual Carbon Footprint: Use Our Calculators," http://www.carbonfund.org/individuals. See also Terrapass, "Calculate Your Carbon Footprint," http://www.terrapass.com/calculate-carbon-footprint/.

9 U.S. Environmental Protection Agency, *Optional Emissions*.

10 For a detailed discussion of aircraft radiative forcing, see Intergovernmental Panel on Climate Change, *Aviation and the Global Atmosphere*, http://www.ipcc.ch/ipccreports/sres/aviation/index.php?idp=64..

11 U.S. Environmental Protection Agency, *Optional Emissions*.

12 Allwood and Cullen, *Sustainable Materials*, 22.

13 Allwood and Cullen, *Sustainable Materials*, 80.

14 For an explanation of the data analysis and data quality, see Geoff P. Hammond and I. Crag Jones, "Embodied Energy and Carbon in Construction Materials," *Proceedings of the Institute of Civil Engineers: Energy*, 161, no. 1 (2008): 87-98, http://www.bath.ac.uk/mech-eng/research/sert/. For the latest data tables see Geoff P. Hammond and I. Crag Jones, "Inventory of Carbon and Energy (ICE) Version 2.0: Summary Tables, January 2011," *Sustainable Energy Research Team, University of Bath*, http://www.siegelstrain.com/site/pdf/ICE-v2.0-summary-tables.pdf.

15 David Simichi-Levi, *Operations Rules: Delivering Customer Value through Flexible Operations*, (Cambridge, MA: The MIT Press, 2010), 203-5.

16 Hammond and Jones, "Embodied Energy and Carbon," 2.

17 Energy and Environmental Analysts, *CHP in the Hotel and Casino Market Sectors*, Prepared for U.S. Environmental Protection Agency, 2005, http://www.epa.gov/chp/documents/hotel_casino_analysis.pdf.

18 U.S. Department of Commerce Bureau of Economic Analysis, *Gross-Domestic-Product-(GDP)-by-Industry Data*, http://www.bea.gov/newsreleases/industry/gdpindustry/gdpindnewsrelease.htm.

19 The EPA reports this figure as 6,702.3 million metric tons, which I converted to U.S. tons. U.S. Environmental Protection Agency, *Inventory of U.S. Greenhouse Gas Emissions and Sinks 1990-2011: Executive Summary*, (ES-26. Washington, DC: EPA, 2013), ES-7, http://www.epa.gov/climatechange/Downloads/ghgemissions/US-GHG-Inventory-2013-ES.pdf.

20 World Bank, "GDP (Current US#) 2009-2013," http://data.worldbank.org/indicator/NY.GDP.MKTP.CD.

21 Allwood and Cullen, *Sustainable Materials*, 80

22 The original report by CNW Marketing Research, titled "Dust to Dust," does not seem to be available online, but you can read reprints of the news story that started the controversy (Chris Demorro, 2007), as well as a number of incredulous responses (e.g., Brendan Koerner). See Chris Demorro, "Prius Outdoes Hummer in Environmental Damage," *The Recorder-Central Connecticut State University*, March 27, 2007, http://www.freerepublic.com/focus/news/1800912/posts. See also Brendan Koerner, Tank vs. hybrid, Slate.com. http://www.slate.com/articles/health_and_science/the_green_lantern/2008/03/tank_vs_hybrid.html.

23 Malcome A. Weiss, John B. Heywood, Elizabeth M. Drake, Andreas Schafer and Felix F. AuYeung, *On the Road in 2020: A Life-cycle Analysis of New Automobile Technologies*, MIT EL 00-003, Cambridge, MA: MIT, 2000. http://web.mit.edu/energylab/www/pubs/el00-003.pdf.

24 Kimberly Aguirre, Luke Eisenhardt, Christian Lim, Brittany Nelson, Alex Norring, Peter Slowik, and Nancy Tu, *Lifecycle Analysis Comparison of Battery Electric Vehicle and a Conventional Gasoline Vehicle*, Prepared for the California Air Resources Board, 7, http://www.environment.ucla.edu/media_IOE/files/BatteryElectricVehicleLCA2012-rh-ptd.pdf.

25 Allwood and Cullen, *Sustainable Materials*, 80.

26 European Commission, *European Platform on Life Cycle Assessment (LCA)*, http://ec.europa.eu/environment/ipp/lca.htm.

Chapter Five: A Carbon Case Study

1 The embodied carbon in materials is presented in CO_2e because the University of Bath dataset does not include CO_2 factors for every material. In this case, the emissions factor for carpet is only given in CO_2e. See Hammond and Jones, *Inventory of Carbon and Energy (ICE).*

Chapter Six: The Green Guide

1 Allwood and Cullen, *Sustainable Materials*, 235.

2 Allwood and Cullen, *Sustainable Materials*, 53.

3 U.S. Department of the Interior, National Park Service, "Environmentally Sustainable Carpet Choices," http://www.nps.gov/sustain/spop/carpet.htm.

4 U.S. Environmental Protection Agency, *SmartWay*, http://www.epa.gov/smartway/.

5 Weber and Matthews, "Food-Miles."

6 Union of Concerned Scientists, *Cooler Smarter*, 150.

7 For example, find advice for pregnant and nursing mothers from Purdue University at Fish4Health.net, as well as a comprehensive guide to sustainable seafood from the Monterey Bay Aquarium. See Purdue University, *Fish4Health.net*, http://fn.cfs.purdue.edu/fish4health/. See also Monterey Bay Aquarium, *Seafood Watch,* http://www.seafoodwatch.org/cr/seafoodwatch.aspx.

Chapter Seven: Get Certified, Go Public

1 Gallup. *Congress and the Public.* http://www.gallup.com/poll/1600/congress-public.aspx.

2 Richard Edleman, "Trust in Government Suffers a Severe Breakdown Across the Globe," *Edelman*, January 23, 2012, http://www.edelman.com/insights/intellectual-property/2012-edelman-trust-barometer/about-trust/press-release/. See also Edelman, Edelman Trust Barometer 2013, http://www.edelman.com/insights/intellectual-property/trust-2013/2013 Edelman Trust Barometer. http://www.edelman.com/insights/intellectual-property/trust-2013/.

3 Edelman, "Trust in Government."

4 Edelman, "Trust in Government."

5 Douglas Vaira, "Win-Win for Wind and wildlife," *The Nature Conservancy*, http://www.nature.org/ourinitiatives/urgentissues/conservationlands/conservation-lands-win-win-for-wind-and-wildlife.xml.

6 Premier Guitar, "Going Green: The Guitar Industry Plans for the Future," *Premier Guitar*, September 9, 2008, http://www.premierguitar.com/articles/going-green-the-guitar-industry-plans-for-the-future-1.

7 See Richard Edelman's remarks about the "dispersion of authority in media" and the necessity of multi-faceted and credible outreach at the International Association of Business Communicators World Conference in 2013. See Richard Edelman, "Go Big or Go Home: My IABC Speech," *Edelman*, http://www.edelman.com/p/6-a-m/the-new-mandate-for-the-communicator/.

8 Makower, *State of Green Business 2013*, 5.

9 Clif Bar & Company provides an excellent case study of relevant and ongoing experience in the company's newsletter. See Elysa Hammond, *Moving Toward Sustainability: Working to Reduce Our Ecological Footprint*, Clif Bar, http://www.clifbar.com/soul/sustainability_newsletter/.

10 U.S. Green Building Council, "Greenbuild International Conference and Expo: Mandatory Exhibition Green Guidelines (GMEGG)," 2013, http://s36.a2zinc.net/clients/usgbc2013/usgbc2013/CUSTOM/Uploads/USGBC13Application.pdf.

11 Convention Industry Council, *APEXASTM Environmentally Sustainable Meeting Standards*, http://www.conventionindustry.org/StandardsPractices/APEXASTM.aspx.

12 International Organization of Standards, *ISO 20121 Event Sustainability Management System*, http://www.iso20121.org.

Chapter Eight: What Does Sustainability Mean?

1 Center for Exhibition Industry Research, *The Cost Effectiveness of Exhibition Participation: Part 1*, http://www.hrsm.sc.edu/travelandtourism/documents/CostEffectivenessof ExhibitionParticipation.pdf.

2 World Commission on Environment and Development, *Our Common Future* (Oxford: Oxford University Press, 1987), http://www.un-documents.net/ocf-02.htm#I.

Conclusion

1 See, for example, the discussion of reducing materials in the structural metal components of buildings in Allwood and Cullen, *Sustainable Materials*, 174.

References

Aguirre, Kimberly, Luke Eisenhardt, Christian Lim, Brittany Nelson, Alex Norring, Peter Slowik, and Nancy Tu. *Lifecycle Analysis Comparison of Battery Electric Vehicle and a Conventional Gasoline Vehicle*. Prepared for the California Air Resources Board. http://www.environment.ucla.edu/media_IOE/files/BatteryElectricVehicleLCA2012-rh-ptd.pdf.

Alley, Richard B. *Earth: The Operators' Manual*. New York: W. W. Norton, 2011.

Allwood, Julian M. and Jonathan M. Cullen. *Sustainable Materials with Both Eyes Open*. Cambridge, England: UTI, 2012.

American Transportation Research Institute. *Estimating Truck-Related Consumption and Emissions in Maine: A Comparative Analysis for a 6-axile, 100,000 Pound Vehicle Configuration*. Agusta: Department of Transportation, 2009. http://www.maine.gov/mdot/ofbs/documents/pdf/atrimainereport.pdf

Bowman, Tom. "Ask Mr. Green: We Are Considering Buying Lightweight Exhibits to Make them More Sustainable." *Exhibitor*, December 2013. http://www.exhibitoronline.com/topics/article.asp?ID=1517&catID=101#.Ut8izKWtu2w.

Bowman, Tom. "Are Businesses Still Earning an Eco-Advantage? With Andrew Winston." *Climate Report*, February 2, 2013. http://tombowman.com/posts/are-businesses-still-earning-an-eco-advantage/.

Bowman, Tom. "How Can Vineyards Survive the Changing Climate? With Lee Hannah and Steve Matthiasson." *Climate Report*, April 27, 2013. http://tombowman.com/posts/how-can-vineyards-survive-the-changing-climate-with-lee-hannah-and-steve-matthiasson/.

Bowman, Tom. "How Could Our World Change Suddenly? With Richard Alley." Climate Report, January 25, 2014. http://tombowman.com/posts/how-could-our-world-change-suddenly-with-richard-alley/.

CarbonFund.org. "Reduce Your Individual Carbon Footprint: Use Our Calculators." http://www.carbonfund.org/individuals.

Center for Exhibition Industry Research. *The Cost Effectiveness of Exhibition Participation: Part 1.* http://www.hrsm.sc.edu/travelandtourism/documents/CostEffectivenessof ExhibitionParticipation.pdf.

Chouinard, Yvon. "On Corporate Responsibility for Planet Earth." *Patagonia.* http://www.patagonia.com/us/patagonia.go?assetid=2386.

Hammond, Elysa. *Moving Toward Sustainability: Working to Reduce Our Ecological Footprint.* Clif Bar. http://www.clifbar.com/soul/sustainability_newsletter/.

Climate Registry. http://www.theclimateregistry.org.

Convention Industry Council. *APEX/ASTM Environmentally Sustainable Meeting Standards.* http://www.conventionindustry.org/StandardsPractices/APEXASTM.aspx.

Convention Industry Council. *The Economic Significance of Meetings to the U.S. Economy: Executive Summary*, February 2011. http://www.conventionindustry.org/Libraries/ESS/CIC_Final_Report_Executive_Summary.sflb.ashx.

Cunningham, Wayne. "Chevy Tahoe Hybrid Wins Green Car of the Year Award." *C/net*, November 15, 2007. http://reviews.cnet.com/8301-13746_7-9818120-48.html.

Cusick, Daniel. "Awareness of Climate Costs, Risks Builds among Major Companies—Survey." *ClimateWire*, January 22, 2014. http://www.eenews.net/climatewire/2014/01/22/stories/1059993249.

Demorro, Chris. "Prius Outdoes Hummer in Environmental Damage." The Recorder-Central Connecticut State University, March 27, 2007. http://www.freerepublic.com/focus/news/1800912/posts.

Edelman. *Edelman Trust Barometer 2013.* http://www.edelman.com/insights/intellectual-property/trust-2013/2013 Edelman Trust Barometer. http://www.edelman.com/insights/intellectual-property/trust-2013/.

Edleman, Richard. "Trust in Government Suffers a Severe Breakdown Across the Globe." *Edelman*, January 23, 2012. http://www.edelman.com/insights/intellectual-property/2012-edelman-trust-barometer/about-trust/press-release/.

Edelman, Richard. "Go Big Or Go Home: My IABC Speech." *Edelman.* http://www.edelman.com/p/6-a-m/the-new-mandate-for-the-communicator/.

Energy and Environmental Analysts. *CHP in the Hotel and Casino Market Sectors*, Prepared for U.S. Environmental Protection Agency, 2005. http://www.epa.gov/chp/documents/hotel_casino_analysis.pdf.

European Commission. *European Platform on Life Cycle Assessment (LCA).* http://ec.europa.eu/environment/ipp/lca.htm.

Esty, Daniel C. and Andrew S. Winston, *Green to Gold: How Smart Companies Use Environmental Strategy to Innovate, Create Value, and Build Competitive Advantage.* New Haven: Yale University Press, 2006.

Fair Labor Association. "Patagonia."
http://www.fairlabor.org/affiliate/patagonia.

Gallup. *Congress and the Public.*
http://www.gallup.com/poll/1600/congress-public.aspx.

GreenBiz Forum 2013. "Yvon Chouinard: Why There Is No Kinship between Apple and Patagonia." *GreenBiz Group.*
http://info.greenbiz.com/SOGB2014Download_ThankYou.html?aliId=48675010.

Greenpeace. "Ask Nestlè CEO to Stop Buying Palm Oil from Destroyed Rainforest." *YouTube.com.*
https://www.youtube.com/watch?v=1BCA8dQfGi0.

Griffen, Paul A. and Yuan Sun. "Going Green: Market Reaction to CSR Newswire Releases." *Social Science Research Network*, January 29, 2012.
http://ssrn.com/abstract=1995132.

Hammond, Geoff P. and I. Crag Jones. "Embodied Energy and Carbon in Construction Materials." *Proceedings of the Institute of Civil Engineers: Energy*, 161, no. 1 (2008): 87-98.
http://www.bath.ac.uk/mech-eng/research/sert/.

Hammond, Geoff P. and I. Crag Jones. "Inventory of Carbon and Energy (ICE) Version 2.0: Summary Tables, January 2011." *Sustainable Energy Research Team, University of Bath.*
http://www.siegelstrain.com/site/pdf/ICE-v2.0-summary-tables.pdf

Hannah, Lee, Patrick R. Roehrdanz, Makihiko Ikegami, Anderson V. Shepard, M. Rebecca Shaw, Gary Tabor, Lu Zhi, Pablo A. Marquet and Robert J. Hijmans. "Climate Change, Wine and Conservation." *Proceedings of the National Academy of Sciences of the United States of America*, 110, no. 17 (2013): 6907-6912.
http://www.pnas.org/content/early/2013/04/03/1210127110.full.pdf+html.

Intergovernmental Panel on Climate Change. *Aviation and the Global Atmosphere.*
http://www.ipcc.ch/ipccreports/sres/aviation/index.php?idp=64.

International Organization of Standards. *ISO 20121 Event Sustainability Management System.*
http://www.iso20121.org.

Ionescu-Somers, Arleen and Albrecht Enders. "How Nestle Dealt with a Social Media Campaign Against It." *Financial Times*, December 3, 2012.
http://www.ft.com/intl/cms/s/0/90dbff8a-3aea-11e2-b3f0-00144feabdc0.html#axzz2rL5pX2IA.

Koerner, Brenda,. Tank vs. hybrid. *Slate.com.*
http://www.slate.com/articles/health_and_science/the_green_lantern/2008/03/tank_vs_hybrid.html.

MacKay, David J. C. *Sustainable Energy: Without Hot Air—Ten-Page Synopsis*. Cambridge: UIT, 2008.
http://withouthotair.com/synopsis10.pdf.

Makower, Joel. *State of Green Business 2013*. Oakland: GreenBiz Group, 2013.
http://info.greenbiz.com/rs/greenbizgroup/images/state-green-business-2013.pdf?mkt_tok=3RkMMJWWfF9wsRonv6%2FKZKXonjHpfsX%2F7%

Monterey Bay Aquarium. *Seafood Watch.*
http://www.seafoodwatch.org/cr/seafoodwatch.aspx.

National Research Council. *Informing Decisions in a Changing Climate*. Washington, DC: The National Academies Press, 2009.

National Research Council. *Technologies and Approaches to Reducing the Fuel Consumption of Medium- and Heavy-Duty Vehicles*. Washington, DC: The National Academies Press, 2010.

Northeast States Center for a Clean Air Future. *Reducing Heavy-Duty Long Haul Combination Truck Fuel Consumption and CO_2 Emissions*. Boston: NESCCAF, 2009. http://www.nesccaf.org/documents/reducing-heavy-duty-long-haul-combination-truck-fuel-consumption-and-co2-emissions.

Ogburn, Michael, Laurie Ramroth and Amory B. Lovins. *Transformational Trucks: Determining the Energy Efficiency Limits of a Class-8 Tractor-Trailer*. Boulder: Rocky Mountain Institute, 2008. http://www.rmi.org/Knowledge-Center/Library/T08-08_TransformationalTrucksEnergyEfficiency.

Pappas, Charles. "HP's Lean, Green Exhibit Machine." *Exhibitor*, 2008. http://www.exhibitoronline.com/topics/article.asp?ID=306&catID=37#.UvfMGaWnnD8.

Pappas, Charles. "Heidelberg's Green Machine." *Exhibitor*, December 2013. http://www.exhibitoronline.com/topics/article.asp?ID=1511#.UuBnZ6Wtu2w.

Patagonia. *FAQs*. http://www.patagonia.com/us/patagonia.go?assetid=67517.

Premier Guitar. "Going Green: The Guitar Industry Plans for the Future." *Premier Guitar*, September 9, 2008. http://www.premierguitar.com/articles/going-green-the-guitar-industry-plans-for-the-future-1.

Purdue University. *Fish4Health.net*. http://fn.cfs.purdue.edu/fish4health/.

Simichi-Levi, David. *Operations Rules: Delivering Customer Value through Flexible Operations*. Cambridge, MA: The MIT Press, 2010.

Stanton, Travis. "As a Matter of Fact." *Exhibitor*, June 2008. http://www.exhibitoronline.com/exhibitormagazine/june08/editorial0608.asp#.Ut75K6Wtu2w.

Southern California Edison, "The Elusive Enemies of Efficiency in the Home." *Energy Vampires*. https://www.scehomeenergyadvisor.com/learn/vampire.

Terrapass. "Calculate Your Carbon Footprint." http://www.terrapass.com/calculate-carbon-footprint/.

The Union of Concerned Scientists. *Cooler Smarter: Practical Steps for Low-Carbon Living*. Washington, DC: Island Press, 2012.

U.N. Framework Convention on Climate Change. "Milestones on the road to 2012: The Cancun Agreements." *United Nations*, 2012. https://unfccc.int/key_steps/cancun_agreements/items/6132.php.

U.S. Census Bureau (website). *State & County QuickFacts*. http://quickfacts.census.gov/qfd/states/00000.html.

U.S. Department of Commerce Bureau of Economic Analysis. *Gross-Domestic-Product-(GDP)-by-Industry Data.* http://www.bea.gov/newsreleases/industry/gdpindustry/gdpindnewsrelease.htm.

U.S. Department of the Interior, National Park Service. "Environmentally Sustainable Carpet Choices." http://www.nps.gov/sustain/spop/carpet.htm.

U.S. Environmental Protection Agency. *Green Vehicle Guide.* http://www.epa.gov/greenvehicles/Index.do;jsessionid=yQTqSp3TW0djjh197LTzf7S91vf0J1c1kwBd6nGDNNNvxQT3120p!1789104575.

U.S. Environmental Protection Agency. *Greenhouse Gas Emissions from a Typical Passenger Vehicle,* EPA-420-F-11-041. Washington, DC: EPA, 2011. http://www.epa.gov/otaq/climate/documents/420f11041.pdf.

U.S. Environmental Protection Agency. *Inventory of U.S. Greenhouse Gas Emissions and Sinks 1990-2011: Executive Summary,* ES-26. Washington, DC: EPA, 2013. http://www.epa.gov/climatechange/Downloads/ghgemissions/US-GHG-Inventory-2013-ES.pdf.

U.S. Environmental Protection Agency. *Optional Emissions from Commuting, Business Travel and Product Transport: Climate Leaders Greenhouse Gas Inventory Protocol Core Module Guidance,* EPA430-R-08-006. Washington, DC: EPA, 2008. http://www.epa.gov/climateleadership/documents/resources/commute_travel_product.pdf.

U.S. Environmental Protection Agency. *SmartWay.* http://www.epa.gov/smartway/.

U.S. Green Building Council. "Greenbuild International Conference and Expo: Mandatory Exhibition Green Guidelines (GMEGG)." 2013. http://s36.a2zinc.net/clients/usgbc2013/usgbc2013/CUSTOM/Uploads/USGBC13Application.pdf.

Vaira, Douglas. "Win-Win for Wind and Wildlife." *The Nature Conservancy.* http://www.nature.org/ourinitiatives/urgentissues/conservationlands/conservation-lands-win-win-for-wind-and-wildlife.xml.

Valentry, Lena. "Trash talk." *Exhibitor.* 2010. http://www.exhibitoronline.com/topics/article.asp?ID=1242&catID=71#.UuBn_6Wtu2w.

Weber, Christopher L, and H. Scott Matthews. "Food-Miles and the Relative Climate Impacts of Food Choices in the United States." *Environmental Science and Technology,* 42. No. 10 (2008): 3508-3513. http://psufoodscience.typepad.com/psu_food_science/files/es702969f.pdf.

Weiss, Malcome A., John B. Heywood, Elizabeth M. Drake, Andreas Schafer and Felix F. AuYeung. *On the Road in 2020: A Life-cycle Analysis of New Automobile Technologies,* MIT EL 00-003. Cambridge, MA: MIT, 2000. http://web.mit.edu/energylab/www/pubs/el00-003.pdf.

World Bank. "GDP (Current US#) 2009-2013." http://data.worldbank.org/indicator/NY.GDP.MKTP.CD.

World Commission on Environment and Development. *Our Common Future.* Oxford: Oxford University Press, 1987. http://www.un-documents.net/ocf-02.htm#I.

Acknowledgements

A book isn't possible without the hard work and generosity of many people. Thanks to a team of dedicated folks for their help with the research: Peter Breaux, Jim Cain, Alex Gjonovich, Jake Huttner, Ray Kuhar, Erin Nichols, Teri Metcalf and Gail Mutke. I owe special thanks to Lee Harrington for creating the space that allowed me to take on this project.

Thanks to those in the meetings and events industry who shared their experiences and passion. They provided counsel and perspectives about sustainable solutions for their businesses and clients. Jeff Baker, Mary Carey, Mike Ellis, David King, Timothy Morris and Karl Pfalzgraf have been especially helpful. I owe a great deal to Mike Field, Ed Hackley and Geoff Siodmak for guiding me into the industry and teaching me how the supplier side works. I am also indebted to clients who taught me about the challenges and opportunities they confront daily.

Thanks to Lee Knight and Travis Stanton for the opportunity to hone my thinking through a monthly column. Thanks, also, to Jeff Provost, Justin Hersh and Paul Salinger for pushing sustainability within the supplier community. Thanks, too, for the opportunity to be part of it.

Quite a few eminent scholars have been generous with their time and expertise over the years. Explaining real science and putting research into practice would not have been possible without their training and guidance. They include Rob Gould, Daniel Koshland, Jon Krosnick, Patrice Legro, Anthony Leiserowitz, Ed Maibach, Michael Mann, Richard Somerville, Jerry Schubel, Peter Schultz, Barry Seltser, Erika Shugart, Debbie Zmarzly and many others.

Writing is a team sport. I owe thanks to Tina Bowman, Rob Gould, Susan Hanley and Tom Van Zandt. This book is much better because of their contributions. Even so, I am responsible for any errors.

Index

20809771R00103

Made in the USA
San Bernardino, CA
24 April 2015